Bearded Dragon Manual

3rd Edition

Philippe de Vosjoli,
Robert Mailloux, Susan Donoghue, VMD,
Roger Klingenberg, DVM, and Jerry Cole

The Bearded Dragon Manual 3rd Edition

CompanionHouse Books™ is an imprint of Fox Chapel Publishing.

Project Team
Editorial Director: Gretchen Bacon
Technical Editor, 3rd Edition: Susan M. Ewing
Technical Editor, 2nd Edition: Terri Sommella
Editor: Amy Deputato
Designer: Mary Ann Kahn
Proofreader/Indexer: Jean Bissell

ISBN 978-1-62008-406-9

Library of Congress Control Number: 2021949757

Fox Chapel Publishing
903 Square Street
Mount Joy, PA 17552

www.facebook.com/companionhousebooks

We are always looking for talented authors. To submit an idea, please send a brief inquiry to acquisitions@foxchapelpublishing.com.

Printed and bound in China
25 24 23 22   2 4 6 8 10 9 7 5 3 1

CONTENTS

INTRODUCTION

I'm a relative newcomer to bearded dragons, but I have quickly fallen under their spell, in part because of a young beardie I met at a local pet shop. "Spike" definitely knew I was on the other side of the glass. He ignored his roommates and clearly wanted to interact with me, and I felt a twinge of sadness at having to leave him there. Obviously, this little guy had personality. I am not alone in feeling drawn to these charming lizards. I join almost two million households in the United States who find that bearded dragons make wonderful pets.

A recent study by the American Pet Products Association reported that 4.5 million households in the United States owned reptiles. A later article in *Reptile Magazine* by John Virata stated that of all the reptiles owned by U.S. households, 40 percent of them were bearded dragons, for a total of 1.8 million households. In all probability, many of these households have more than one bearded dragon. That's a lot of dragons!

One thing to consider if you plan to get a bearded dragon is that bearded dragons are not "beginner" pets. You need to be prepared for your dragon *before* you get him. Don't bring a beardie home and then decide you need to learn about him! Bearded dragons have very specific temperature and dietary requirements, and they need a moderately large space to call home. They may not be as demonstrative as a dog or cat, but they definitely have personalities, and they do bond with their owners. Because they don't have fur, they may be ideal for those with allergies. And they come in a wonderful assortment of colors, or "morphs." I still can't decide which is my favorite.

An advantage to owning a bearded dragon as opposed to another type of reptile is that beardies are all captive-bred. When you buy a bearded dragon, you are not buying an animal that has been taken from its native habitat, with all the stress that implies. *Captive-bred* means you are getting a calmer animal and an affordable price.

On that note, it's interesting that the United States is the largest importer and exporter of reptiles, according to John Virata's aforementioned article. Captive breeding, with more than 10,000 hobby breeders, "has made the United States the major exporter of species that are not even native to North America." Reptile breeding has gone from a hobby to a business worth more than a billion dollars annually.

With the expertise of renowned herpetologist Philippe de Vosjoli, top reptile veterinarians, and accomplished bearded dragon breeders, *Bearded Dragon Manual* has been a staple in the libraries of those who love this fascinating lizard. Now in an updated third edition, this comprehensive volume continues to offer essential, detailed information to bearded-dragon beginners and experienced fanciers alike. This expanded edition features a new chapter on training and enrichment as well as some "just for fun" tidbits for bearded dragon keepers. We hope you enjoy the delight, wonder, and discovery you will encounter as you bond with your bearded dragon.

Susan M. Ewing,
former "Pet Pen" columnist,
The Post-Journal of Jamestown, NY

CHAPTER 1

GENERAL INFORMATION

COMMON NAME	SPECIES NAME
Inland bearded dragon	*P. vitticeps*
Eastern bearded dragon	*P. barbata*
Rankins or Lawson's dragon	*P. henrylawsoni*

Note: Hybrids of the Eastern bearded dragon and Lawson's dragon are called Vittikin dragons.

"Bearded dragon" is the common name applied to lizards of the genus *Pogona* in the family Agamidae, several of which display a beard-like extension of the throat, which turns black when threatened. The bearded dragon most readily available to pet owners is the inland bearded dragon (*P. vitticeps*). Because the inland bearded dragon is by far the most popular, the information presented in this book relates to that species unless indicated otherwise.

Two other types of bearded dragon are commercially bred in very small numbers: *Pogona henrylawsoni*, otherwise known as Rankins dragon, is shorter than its inland cousin and has a blunter snout. It is also called Lawson's dragon, Black Soil bearded dragon, Dumpy bearded dragon, and Pygmy dragon. Rankins dragon is smaller and more manageable than its larger cousin, and needs much less space (15-gallon [57L] enclosure versus 120-gallon [454L] enclosure). Rankins dragons are rare in the United States because of a very small gene pool. They are all descended from dragons imported illegally, so there is no new blood being introduced. As well, it does not reproduce as easily as the inland bearded dragon and thus is not readily available. The *Pogona barbata*, the common, or Eastern, bearded dragon, is found in wooded areas of Australia and is arboreal. It is more aggressive than *P. vitticeps* and is rarely offered for sale because it also has proven difficult to breed consistently and presents certain problems in long-term husbandry that still need to be resolved.

Eastern bearded dragon

Other species of bearded dragons include the *Pogona minor minima*, called the Abrolhos bearded, or Abrolhos dwarf bearded, dragon. These cousins of the inland dragon are smaller, being only about 8 inches (20cm) long, including the tail. They are named for the chain of islands where they are found—the Houtman Abrolhos—a group of islands off the western coast of Australia. The dragons are found on four of the 122 islands in the chain.

Pogona microlepidota, or the Kimberly bearded dragon, is rarely found outside of its home in western Australia and is another smaller dragon. *Pogona minor mitchelli*, or the Northwest bearded dragon, is rarely seen outside its native Australia and rarely ever kept as a pet. This is also true of *Pogona nullarbori*. The Nullarbor bearded dragon is named for the region in which it is found, the Nullarbor Plain in southern Australia.

Bearded dragons come in a variety of morphs, including normal brown-and-tan dragons. There are colors such as citrus, red, and orange, and "zero" dragons who are gray, silver, or white. They have no color or pattern. Hypomelanistic dragons can come in any color, but the color is lighter. A hypomelanistic dragon will have clear nails rather than black ones. In translucent dragons, the skin looks a bit translucent, and their colors tend to be quite strong. Sometimes translucent dragons have normal eyes, and sometimes one eye is black and the other is normal, but translucent dragons mainly tend to have black eyes.

Bearded dragons also have different textures. Normal beardies have stiff scales all over their bodies. Leatherback bearded dragons have smooth skin, with spikes only on the beard and along the stomach. Dunners have scales going in all different directions instead of all pointing the same way. A leatherback Dunner will have smooth, leathery skin, but the scales on the beard and sides will be going in different directions. Paradox dragons have no easily detectable pattern or color, and they sometimes look as if someone splashed them with

An example of a red-orange dragon.

A dragon with blue coloration.

Bearded dragons are easy for children to handle if done properly.

paint. Dragons may also be designated by the type of markings, such as blue bar or tiger stripe, and breeders continue to develop new morphs for an even wider variety of bearded dragons.

IS A BEARDED DRAGON THE RIGHT PET FOR YOU?

When it comes to costs, the bearded dragon is not a beginner pet. A bearded dragon needs planning, and you really need to be ready for your bearded dragon before he comes home. You must have a heat- and humidity-controlled habitat prepared ahead of time, and your bearded dragon must go into this habitat as soon as you bring him home. Costs of equipment and supplies will vary, but be prepared for an initial outlay of about $400 to $500, including the cost of the bearded dragon. Once your dragon is settled in, you'll have the monthly costs of food and supplements, and you should have a budget for the occasional veterinary visit if needed.

The cost of the bearded dragon itself will vary depending on where you get your beardie and what particular morph you choose. A rare color or pattern can add several hundred dollars to your initial expenses. Bearded dragons in a pet store, even those termed "fancy," are likely to be cheaper than a dragon from a breeder. Depending on the pet store, employees may or may not know anything about the care and feeding of a bearded dragon. If you buy from a reputable breeder, however, he or she will be a good source of information and should be able to help with any questions you have after your purchase. Research breeders before you buy! Bearded dragons are relatively easy to breed, and a beardie owner who happens to hatch a clutch of eggs may not be any more knowledgeable than you are.

First and foremost, you will need somewhere for your new pet to live. If you are getting a juvenile bearded dragon, you'll start off with a 20-gallon (76L) long tank. Try to find one on sale or used, because you'll soon need to upgrade to a larger

Did You Know?

Many customers who cannot or do not want to feed live insects will feed black soldier fly larvae, available under various brand names. They can be kept in the cup in which they are shipped, do not need to be fed or refrigerated, and have a shelf life of two to three weeks.

tank for your adult beardie, who needs an enclosure of at least 48 inches long by 24 inches deep (wide) by 24 inches high (122 x 61 x 61cm).

For the enclosure, you'll need a heat source and a dome to direct the heat downward. Bearded dragons also need UVB light, which is necessary for their well-being and proper digestion. A linear UVB bulb should cover two-thirds of the habitat area. You will need a hood for the bulb, and plan to replace the bulb every six months.

If the temperature in your tank will drop below 70°F (21°C) at night, you will need a heat emitter. This is a bulb that emits heat but no light, so it won't disturb your dragon at night.

A combination thermometer/hydrometer ensures that the temperature and humidity, respectively, stay in the correct range. Also invest in a temperature gun, which will help you get an accurate reading of the temperature on the basking shelf.

A basking shelf can cost you nothing if you build your own from sterilized rocks or branches, but even a purchased structure should not be too expensive. You'll also need a hut for your beardie to hide in. Place it on the cooler side of the tank. Avoid a natural wood hut, as these are usually made of pine, which is not good for your dragon.

If you're getting a young dragon, cover the tank floor with paper towels, which are inexpensive and make cleanup easy. Once your juvenile has graduated to his permanent home, you can continue using paper towels or switch to non-adhesive shelf paper or even tiles, which many owners like because they can help keep the dragon's nails worn down. Tiles are an inexpensive option if you have your own tile cutter.

Feeding and supplementation are other expenses. A food bowl simply needs to be sturdy and have sides to contain bugs and worms; you may already have something

A proper bearded dragon setup recreates certain aspects of its wild habitat.

Young dragons in their habitat, complete with basking area and plenty of natural features.

suitable. Feeding a baby dragon costs about five times what feeding an adult costs, and you can lower your feed costs by raising your own crickets and/or Dubia roaches. Otherwise, it is cheaper to have your bugs shipped to you than to buy them from a pet store. You'll also need D3 and a vitamin mixture, but a standard-size container of each should last almost a year.

Cleaning supplies are fairly simple and should not cost much. You can find a spray bottle at a dollar store and make your own cleaning solution out of water and vinegar.

Bearded dragons benefit from a daily soak, so get a bottle of a water conditioner such as ReptiSafe™ from your local pet-supply store. This product neutralizes the effect of chlorine in your tap water and makes it safe for your beardie to soak in and drink.

Be prepared for an initial outlay of several hundred dollars, not including the cost of the bearded dragon, to start. Many of these are one-time expenses, and then you'll just have monthly food costs. Don't forget to budget for veterinary visits. An annual exam is a good idea, you'll also need to visit the vet if your beardie is sick or injured.

Having said all that, bearded dragons are beautiful, active, entertaining, moderately sized, easy to handle, naturally tame (with few exceptions), and relatively easy to keep. Compared to smaller reptiles, they are robust and hardy. Compared to larger reptiles, they are relatively safe for children, although basic hygiene habits such as hand-washing must be practiced.

Size

Baby inland bearded dragons are just under 4 inches (10cm) when born and weigh about 1/10 ounce (2.5 to 3g). The length of adult dragons is typically 17 to 23 inches (43 to 58cm), and they weigh at least ¾ pound (340g).

Because bearded dragons require substantial amounts of food, including live insects, they defecate frequently, so their enclosures and substrates have to be cleaned daily. Of course, there are ways to minimize the amount of time that cleanup takes. Using paper towels as a substrate makes cleanup fast and easy, but some owners may prefer the look of reptile carpet.

Although bearded dragons seem to present less risk of disease transmission than some other reptiles, you must practice simple hygiene if you are to share your home with a bearded dragon. Any reptile can carry the *Salmonella* bacterium, which can be shed in the feces and may pose a disease threat to humans, especially infants, toddlers, and those who are immune suppressed. You should never allow your bearded dragon on food-handling surfaces, such as kitchen counters and dining-room tables. You should wash your hands immediately after handling your bearded dragon. Wash your dragon's food and water bowls separately from your household dishes. And, of course, keep your bearded dragon's enclosure scrupulously clean. Sound judgment and common sense will keep your dragon a low-risk, valued member of the household.

NATURAL HABITAT

All bearded dragons originated in Australia. Although dragons currently found in the pet trade are many generations removed from their Australian roots, details about their habitat in the wild provide clues to proper husbandry in captivity.

Most bearded dragons live in relatively hot, arid regions of Australia, and thus require a warm, dry enclosure in captivity. However, water is mandatory and should be offered in shoulder-deep water bowls, through misting and/or soaking (depending on the age of the animal), and through fresh greens. A bearded dragon's enclosure should offer temperature gradients, meaning that the dragon should be able to move from the hot basking side of the tank to the cooler side to lower its internal temperature when necessary.

Wild bearded dragons in Australia enjoy climbing and basking on rock piles and on the rails and posts of fences. When designing a home for your juvenile dragon, include a long,

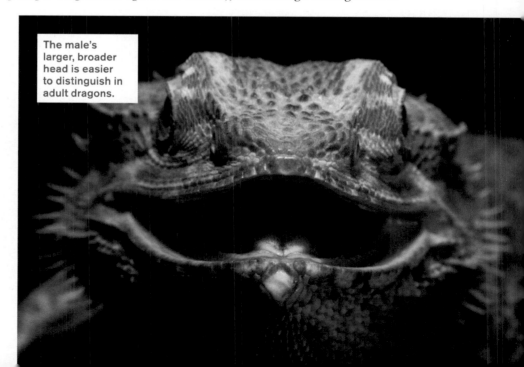

The male's larger, broader head is easier to distinguish in adult dragons.

Pogona minor minima

low, smooth rock—natural or artificial. For an adult, a large, thick piece of driftwood will act as a climbing branch and be happily accepted. Provide a basking light so the dragon can heat up, which stimulates feeding.

LONGEVITY

Although there are a few reports of pet inland bearded dragons exceeding ten years of age, most live between five and eight years if they are initially healthy and raised in good conditions.

It is easy to fall in love with bearded dragons, but loving a bearded dragon is not enough when it comes to giving your pet the care it needs and deserves. Being an excellent caregiver is what will give your dragon the potential to reach its maximum life expectancy. The fact that you purchased this book says that you are well on your way to understanding your bearded dragon's needs and providing an environment that meets those needs.

SEXING

Accurately determining the sex of baby bearded dragons is difficult; at best, it is an educated guess. Adults, however, show secondary sexual characteristics that allow for relatively easy sexual identification.

When trying to sex juvenile bearded dragons, people often examine several factors. The first trait to look at is the tail taper. The tails of females taper more sharply from the base compared to those of males, which appear just slightly thicker. This method is most successful when applied to the small percentage

A young Lawson's dragon.

of individuals that show greater extremes of tail taper. The differences in tail taper often become more pronounced as bearded dragons grow older.

The femoral pores are examined next. Prominent femoral pores on a 6-inch (15cm) juvenile would indicate a probable male. Femoral pores show as a running line of dots on the inner thighs of the dragons.

Head size is also possibly helpful in determining the sex of babies because males tend to have a wider skull base compared to females. This is not always true but, combined with the aforementioned methods, looking at the skull's width can help you determine the probable sex of a baby bearded dragon.

Another technique has improved the accuracy of sexing small bearded dragons, but it must be performed with extreme care and is best done by an expert dragon handler. This method consists of holding a dragon facing out and lying flat on the palm of one hand while gently bending the dragon's tail above the body plane with the other hand. You *must* perform this task gently. Carefully bending the tail toward the ceiling, above the body plane, will cause the skin on the ventral side (underside) of the tail base to be stretched back, which will show the outlines of hemipenal bulges in males. These bulges run directly caudal (toward the tail) from the vent (cloacal opening). A defined, central post-anal groove—two vertical bulges with a channel running between—is a good indicator of a male. In females, slight post-anal bulges may be visible, but they tend to run laterally from the vent, midline, like the arms of an inverted "V." A probable female can appear flat right above the vent or can show one small bump. This method works best with experience and is usually complemented by other concurring observations, such as the male's thicker tail and wider cloacal opening.

When sexing subadult and adult bearded dragons, you can apply the same method of raising the tail as described for sexing babies. As with babies, extreme gentleness is a must. Subadult and adult dragons can also be accurately sexed by pulling back the vent flap and exposing the cloacal opening. In males, the

German Giants

The German Giant morph was known to reach up to 26 inches (66cm) in length. While true German Giants are gone from the genetic pool in the United States, some lines still advertise this morph in their genetic mix, although it is likely to be many generations removed. If true German Giant size is important to you, request the sizes of the parents of offspring you are considering. This way, you should be able to tell if any German Giant remains in that breeder's line or at least in those two parents.

cloacal opening is significantly wider and larger than in females. Assessing the cloacal opening in babies is ineffective because males need to be older before the greater cloacal width becomes clearly noticeable.

In an adult male, you can evert one of the hemipenes by applying pressure with a thumb to one side of the tail base and rolling up toward the vent, which should cause a hemipenis to protrude. This process requires experience to perform properly and is sometimes applied to determine the sex of small bearded dragons, but it is not recommended because of the high risk of injury from crushing trauma if not performed with the proper level of experience and sensitivity. It is usually unnecessary to go to extremes to determine the sex of adults.

Many adults are also easy to sex from secondary sexual characteristics, including the aforementioned thicker tails/less tail taper and enlarged femoral pores in males. Also, adult males develop larger and broader heads as they mature. Males will also "display," which means they show a dark throat (beard) and head-bobbing behavior, especially during the breeding season.

LIFE STAGES

Bearded dragons undergo six life stages. Understanding these life stages is important to successfully raising and maintaining bearded dragons for long, happy lives. The six life stages, with corresponding sizes and/or ages, are as follows:

1. **Embryonic/prebirth (fifty-five to seventy-five days):** In captivity, this period of development, which occurs within the confines of the egg, is usually spent in an incubator. However, genetics, diet, health of the mother, and incubation conditions can all play roles in health at this stage.
2. **Hatchling (birth to about 5 inches [13cm]):** Newly hatched babies are acclimating to life outside the egg. The first few days are a rest period and then, over the following few weeks, babies learn to drink, find small prey, and develop a routine of basking, eating, and sleeping.
3. **Juvenile (5 to 13 inches [13 to 33cm]:** Stages 2 and 3 are characterized by ravenous appetite, frequent feeding, rapid growth, and a tendency to mutilate other young dragons, including nipping

off tail tips, toes, or other low extremities, when food is insufficient. If the babies are hungry enough, they may even try to eat each other completely, not just the extremities.

Eating and growing are the primary concerns of Stage 3. In this stage, dragons frequently perform arm-waving behavior, a type of appeasement and intraspecies identity display. A social hierarchy based on feeding vigor/assertion and growth develops into two levels: the tough, big, aggressive feeders and the shy, small, "feed after the others" individuals.

The primary differences between Stages 3 and 4 (subadult) are size and behavior. Stage 3 begins when the young dragons reach a length of 5 to 6 inches (13 to 16cm). Mutilation tendencies toward animals in the same size range continue. By Stage 4, cannibalistic tendencies greatly decrease, as does the frequency of arm waving, especially in males. Dragons grow rapidly and eat a greater percentage of plant matter. A pattern develops: the bigger a dragon grows, the more it eats, so the more it grows, and so on. Social behaviors are still limited and, if enough food is provided, mostly passive.

These tendencies to munch on each other if there isn't enough food is one of the reasons, should you decide to have more than one beardie or hatch a clutch, that each dragon must have its own habitat. Smaller babies can be temporarily housed in smaller spaces until they have grown to 5 inches (13cm) or so.

4. **Subadult/adult (13 to 22 inches [33 to 56cm]):** Stage 4 lasts through the first three years of breeding activity. This socially interactive stage is characterized by a greater range of social behaviors, which are triggered by sexual maturity. The onset of sexual social behaviors results in well-defined hierarchies, with an alpha male becoming ruler of the roost. Males perform courtship, territorial, aggressive, and breeding behaviors. Females perform slow

Baby bearded dragons acclimate to life inside their enclosure.

head-bobbing behaviors or push-ups to reveal their identity. Females also display submissive arm-waving behaviors during breeding. Growth rates at this stage decline because of hormonal changes and the diversion of energy and nutrients away from growth and toward breeding. Dragons achieve their adult length during this stage. The second year of Stage 4 will bring an increase in girth but usually no increase in length. After the onset of Stage 4, bearded dragons normally go through a brumation (winter shutdown period) annually.

5. **Mature adult (fourth year of breeding until five or six years old):** A gradual decrease in reproductive rate and little, if any, significant growth are associated with this stage of a bearded dragon's life, which lasts two to three years.

6. **Old age (usually by six to seven years of age):** This stage is characterized by little or no breeding, at least in females. There is no measurable growth. Eventually, old bearded dragons enter a terminal stage of decreased feeding and increased lethargy that, over weeks or months, leads to death. It is wise to cut back on calories (but not all nutrients) with old dragons and pay special attention to providing adequate levels of water as well as comfortable surroundings and stress-free days.

HOW FAST DO BEARDED DRAGONS GROW?

In one instance, breeders raised a group of baby bearded dragons indoors, using basking lights (basking sites of 95°F [35°C]) and twist Vita-Lite fluorescent full-spectrum bulbs within 6 inches (15cm) of the dragons. They offered insects to the dragons three times a day and had a variety of plant matter available all day. They kept the lights on for sixteen hours daily.

The hatchlings averaged just under 4 inches (10cm) in length at the beginning. After fourteen weeks, the largest specimen had reached a total length of just over 14 inches (36cm). The smallest was 11 inches (28cm) long.

The rate of growth can also be affected by the quality of feeder insects. Another breeder raised babies from hatchling to eight weeks on different feeder insects. They fed one group gut-loaded crickets and greens, and they fed the second group Phoenix Worms® (the original brand of black soldier fly larvae) and leafy greens. They raised both groups under a ReptiSun 10.0 UVB bulb at a distance of 12 inches (31cm). By the end of eight weeks, the cricket-fed group reached an average length of 7 inches (18cm), while the group fed Phoenix Worms reached an average of 9 inches (23cm).

Be sure to find an experienced reptile veterinarian.

As a general guide, under this kind of intensive rearing regimen, growth will average 2 to 2½ inches (5 to 6cm) a month for the first six months, and males can reach sexual maturity as early as five to six months of age. The growth rate begins to taper off after about six months.

Kept in optimal conditions, bearded dragons can grow fast, requiring more food than you may have realized and larger enclosures at an earlier age than you may have planned. Of course, the upside to this fast growth is that within a very short period of time, your bearded dragon can be sitting on your shoulder and becoming more involved with the family.

COMMON HEALTH PROBLEMS

As with many fast-growing lizards, the most common problem seen in immature bearded dragons is calcium deficiency associated with soft bones (metabolic bone disease, or MBD) or with twitches and seizures (low blood calcium, or hypocalcemia). Calcium deficiency results from several factors that may occur singly or together: improper vitamin/mineral supplementation; inadequate heat, which prevents the absorption of calcium supplements; an inappropriate diet or feeding schedule; and insufficient exposure to an ultraviolet-B (UVB) light source.

Two other diseases common in bearded dragons of all ages are caused by parasites. One is heavy pinworm infestation, which remains a significant cause of these lizards' failure to gain or maintain weight. Another, more problematic, disease is coccidiosis, caused by a type of protozoan parasite. Both diseases require diagnosis and treatment by a qualified veterinarian (see Chapter 10).

Older pet dragons may suffer from gout, liver disease, kidney failure, or even cancer. The current knowledge about these disorders suggests that ensuring proper hydration, correct thermal gradients, and an appropriate balanced diet are the best potential preventive measures.

CHAPTER 2

SELECTING YOUR DRAGON

Females can be picky about both food and mates.

Probably nothing is more important for successful bearded-dragon keeping than the initial selection of your animal. You must pay attention and choose, to the best of your abilities, an apparently healthy dragon to start with, or you must work with a reputable breeder who will use his or her experience to choose wisely for you. You should also evaluate what you expect from owning a bearded dragon: is the lizard meant to be a pet that interacts with you, a display animal noted for its beauty, a dragon that will be bred, or some combination of these purposes? Will this dragon live with children? Other family pets? A caring and qualified breeder can help by selecting the right dragon for your situation.

GENDER AND NUMBER OF DRAGONS

Both sexes of bearded dragon make good pets, but males grow larger and are considered by some to exhibit more character, personality, and responsiveness. Of the color morphs, males tend to be brighter in color than females. Some females are more particular about what they want—"You are feeding me that again today?"—and may run a risk of egg binding. Of course, most people become completely hooked on these lizards, with their winning personalities and with so many colors to choose from, and rapidly wind up with a collection!

After all, if you are going to get one bearded dragon, it doesn't take much more work (and it can be much more entertaining) to keep two or three. Remember, though, that two or three beardies means two or three habitats, as each should have its own space, although you can keep one male and one female together if you plan to breed them.

On that note, how many bearded dragons should you get? If you a want a single pet, an individual bearded dragon will fare well enough, though males may display signs of social deprivation by bobbing their heads at you. This mainly occurs during sexual maturity, and many males calm down as they grow up and become regular coach potatoes. Females can be sweet and charming in their own right.

Because bearded dragons are social creatures, an adult male and female pair, matched so they are close in age and size, is an ideal combination. If you wish to breed, start with juveniles and raise them separately until they are ready to breed; this way, you will have a close bond with both dragons.

Some breeders maintain larger groups, using a ratio of one male to two females. However, in indoor enclosures, a 1:1 ratio is preferable because it reduces the stress of the breeding animals. In the 1:2 ratio, one female always seems to eat less and is in a more subordinate position.

In large walk-in enclosures, you can keep up to two males and four females together. Although adult males will get into territorial and competitive engagements during the breeding season, they are usually not aggressive enough to cause serious harm to each other. Close observation is nonetheless always

This dragon's belly shows the dark markings associated with stress.

An ideal setup, if you have the space and ability, is to provide each baby with an individual space.

necessary to evaluate the compatibility of dragons kept in a group and prevent potentially dangerous situations.

Baby bearded dragons raised in groups are very competitive and will form hierarchies early on in which the tougher and usually larger animals will intimidate smaller ones and eat most of the food. This causes the dominant dragons to grow faster, making them even more intimidating and dominating. It's a vicious circle. If small specimens are not separated from larger specimens, the small ones will often hide, fare poorly, or eventually become food for their bigger brothers and sisters. It's imperative that you closely observe the dragons to evaluate their individual growth, health, and welfare. As soon as you observe a dominance situation, you should move the submissive babies in with other submissive babies so that they will thrive. You'll then observe the dominance display all over again. Often, babies kept in groups indoors need to be moved every day or sometimes even several times a day so that all of them get the chance to eat and grow.

To prevent mutilation and/or cannibalism among the babies, they should be separated within a few days of hatching. Breeding requires a lot of time, effort, and space and may be more work than you want to take on as a pet owner.

Baby dragons have different personalities and behaviors that affect how they grow up.

PERSONALITY AND INTELLIGENCE

Bearded dragons are like any other pet, such as dogs, cats, horses, and birds, in that they vary in personality. Some are more personable and responsive than others. Some show more signs of intelligence. Some are even spunky and full of attitude from the time they are very young, readily displaying an open mouth in readiness to bite, even right out of the egg! There are very few occurrences of mean adults; the vast majority of bearded dragons are calm and friendly. Bearded dragons can become very attached to their owners, and most will rapidly become a central part of the family, much as a dog or a cat would. They have intriguing qualities and behavior that endears them to most new owners right off the bat. Additionally, for people with fur allergies, a bearded dragon is a perfect alternative.

The intelligence level of bearded dragons has been compared to that of dogs, and, in many cases, this may be true. Adults frequently know their names as well as certain words or phrases, such as "bath

Adding a bearded dragon to the family means committing to its proper care.

What to Avoid

- Do not pick a dragon that remains on the ground with its eyes closed. After brief periods of activity, sick and weak dragons often close their eyes and resume a sluggish posture.

- If most dragons in a tank appear unhealthy, do not buy a dragon from that enclosure. There is a good chance that the sick dragons will have infected the few that still appear healthy.

- Do not pick a thin dragon with a skinny tail and a visible outline of the hipbones.

- Avoid a dragon with depressions in the back of the head.

- Do not select a dragon with fecal smearing around the vent and base of the tail because there is a good chance that it has internal parasites.

- Do not pick a runt or baby whose head appears bulbous in the back. It may eventually grow to be normal, but you would be starting off with an undersized or premature pet.

- Avoid a baby that shows repetitive opening and closing of the mouth and makes light popping sounds; these are signs of a respiratory infection. Do not confuse this, however, with the normal gaping that a dragon performs when it is starting to overheat under a basking light.

- Finally, do not get the misguided notion that you are going to save a poor dragon that is ill, runty, or missing limbs. Most sick-looking baby bearded dragons die. If they don't, there is a good chance that their owners end up spending quite a bit of money on veterinary bills to take care of their health problems. Nature doesn't select for the weakest, and neither should you. If you already have healthy dragons, bringing a sick one home can put them all at risk of contracting a disease.

time" or "food time." Chapter 11 will give you more information on other things bearded dragons can learn. Intelligence and personality are two factors that should be as important in a breeding program as vigor and color.

Bearded dragons become bonded with their people.

SIZE

For a first-time owner, a 6- to 8-inch (15- to 20cm) juvenile that appears to be in good shape is a better long-term survival prospect than a 4-inch (10cm) baby and is well worth the extra cost. If good color is important to you, ask to see photos of the parents and note the genetic line. Keep in mind that juveniles will change color as they grow and shed to adulthood, some quite dramatically. Baby color is not adult color.

Occasionally, breeders offer older dragons past their reproductive prime but with several good years left as pets and family members. Keep in mind, though, that it is very difficult to judge the age of an older bearded dragon. You may be considering what you are told is a two-year-old dragon that is really five years old and will not be with you very long or could cost quite a bit in vet bills.

Selecting a healthy bearded dragon is the first step in a rewarding relationship with your new pet.

SIGNS OF A POTENTIALLY HEALTHY BEARDED DRAGON

Many owners purchase bearded dragons through online breeders. Often, you can get a feel for the quality of a breeder's animals just by assessing his or her website. Prices can also alert you to the difference. As a breeder, it costs a good amount of money to raise high-quality dragons. A good breeder will take the time to coach you before the sale and after your dragon arrives and be available to answer questions in the future.

Price should never be the deciding factor. Remember that you get what you pay for. Many first-time owners will buy the cheapest dragon they can find and then fill up an adult-sized enclosure with hundreds

Good breeders are focused on raising healthy dragons right from the start.

Quarantine

Anyone who purchases one or more dragons and wants to add them to an enclosure with other bearded dragons or to a breeding colony should first quarantine the new lizard(s) individually. Keep the new bearded dragon or dragons in a separate enclosure with newspaper or paper-towel substrate for a period of at least sixty days. During that time, carefully monitor the lizard(s) and have a veterinarian perform fecal exams for parasites. Keep a weekly record of each dragon's weight during this period to assess its growth and health. Diseases of special concern are coccidiosis and pinworm infection, both of which can quickly spread in an established collection. You will save yourself a lot of trouble by establishing quarantine procedures before mixing animals.

of dollars worth of backgrounds, expensive substrates and basking bulbs, a plethora of rock formations, hammocks, and play items. Many of these items are detrimental to the dragon's health by keeping the juvenile under constant stress. This, to me, is like buying a $50 puppy and spending $300 on a leash that chokes the puppy.

Instead, spend as much as you can afford on investing in a good-quality dragon and then simplify the setup. Your dragon (and your bank account) will thank you. Bearded dragon juveniles need only a very simple setup in a 20-gallon (76L) long tank. This allows them to find food easily and make the enclosure their home territory.

If you purchase a dragon at a pet shop or reptile show, there are some things you can look for. Healthy hatchlings may open their mouths and threaten to bite when a large hand approaches them. This is normal behavior for a healthy baby. Babies who appear to be sleeping in your hand may actually be listless and ill.

Look for belly marks, which are dark striations or patterns on the belly of the dragon. These dark markings are a sign of stress. Like people, bearded dragons kept under constant stress will become ill.

Look for an animal with rounded body contours and without visible skeletal outlines, particularly along the hipbones and spine. Make sure that the digits and tail are intact. Your dragon should be bright-eyed and either active or resting comfortably under a basking bulb with its head and upper body raised. It should be bilaterally symmetrical: both eyes should be the same size, and the dragon should not have a kink or bend in its back.

Did You Know?

Help your bearded dragon adjust to his new home with this simple trick. When your beardie arrives from shipping or a local purchase, place white paper around the outside of all four sides of his tank or enclosure. Once his belly marks (striations or a dark pattern on a bearded dragon's stomach, which are a sign of stress) have completely disappeared, remove one sheet of paper per week.

Stressed-out babies are dark and thin.

CHAPTER 3

MAKING A HOME FOR YOUR DRAGON

Allowing a dragon to roam free in your home or even in a single room may appear at first to be a good thing, but what may be perceived as freedom for the lizard can become a death trap.

Dragons that are loose in households fail to keep themselves adequately warm and hydrated and thus can become immune-suppressed, potentially falling ill from infections. Moreover, humans might step on loose dragons, or household dogs and cats may treat them as prey. They may receive serious or fatal electrical shocks from wires or equally serious trauma from toppling books, lamps, and the like. Loose dragons risk setting fires by bringing combustibles, such as curtains, into contact with hot items, such as light bulbs. Responsible bearded dragon owners who are dedicated to providing the best for their pets keep their dragons in appropriate enclosures and let them out only when they can be supervised closely or share time with the family.

ENCLOSURES

Bearded dragons are moderately sized lizards that, as they grow, require larger enclosures. When deciding on an enclosure, it is important to consider the bearded dragon as a two-stage lizard even if you want to invest right away in the larger enclosure it will need when fully grown. The very best size for a 6- to 7-inch (15- to 18cm) juvenile dragon is a 30-inch-long by 12-inch-high (76 x 31cm) enclosure, which is essentially a 20-gallon (76L) long tank. You can keep the dragon in this size tank for about four months after bringing it home. Keeping a baby dragon in a larger enclosure is problematic because the dragon may fail to find its food, water, basking sites, and shelters. He may be overwhelmed by the size of the tank and feel

Consider the number of dragons and their sizes when planning an adequate habitat.

insecure and stressed. The UVB may be placed too high to be effective. As the baby grows, however, you will need to provide a larger enclosure.

The smallest enclosure for one or two adult bearded dragons is either 4 feet long by 2 feet deep (122 x 61cm) or 6 feet long by 18 inches deep (183 x 46cm). A standard 55-gallon (208L) aquarium, which measures 48 inches long by 13 inches deep (122 x 33cm), can house a single adult specimen, but do not go any smaller. A smaller tank will restrict activity in a way that is not optimal for the animal's welfare. Bearded dragons cannot thermoregulate in a tank or enclosure that is too short. Bearded dragons need to adjust their internal temperature accordingly to become hungry, to digest food, and to cool off to prevent death.

The most widely sold enclosures in the reptile trade are all-glass tanks. These are fine for bearded dragons, but there are two potential problems: many stores do not carry the larger sizes, and their size and weight make them challenging to transport. There are also large, lightweight, plastic molded enclosures with sliding glass fronts sold in the reptile trade (e.g., Vision Products) that can be designed for housing bearded dragons. You can order these enclosures online if your local reptile store does not stock them.

Enclosures can come in various materials, including melamine and PVC. As long as you can easily clean and disinfect the habitat, almost any substance will do. (**Note:** Avoid pine wood, which is toxic to bearded dragons.) Doors on the side of the tank are preferred, rather than a top that opens. Hands reaching down are too much like a predator and will frighten and stress your beardie. Also, lighter-colored walls help by reflecting heat.

It is not necessary to go to extremes to maintain a healthy dragon. A simple 48-inch by 24-inch by 24-inch (122 x 61 x 61cm) enclosure for an adult bearded dragon will keep the dragon healthy and happy throughout its life.

Understanding Your Dragon

Starting with a juvenile dragon will give an owner an understanding of a bearded dragon's daily needs. Then, as the dragon grows up, an exhibit can be created around the needs of the dragon that you understand firsthand. Experience is the best teacher.

OUTDOOR SETUPS

In a few warm areas of the United States, such as southern California or some parts of Florida, bearded dragons can be kept in outdoor screened or covered pens year-round as long as they are provided with shelters from rain and have areas of soil or piles of hay to burrow into. In some other areas of the United States, bearded dragons can be kept outdoors in simple pens during the warm months. Breeders

Outdoor Safety

Make sure that an outdoor enclosure for a bearded dragon is secure and covered with a screen or mesh top to prevent escape and to keep out potential predators, such as foxes, raccoons, cats, and birds of prey. If your pen will be in an area with fireflies (lightning bugs), keep in mind that these insects can kill a bearded dragon quickly if ingested.

Bearded dragons like bright enclosures that let in as much light as possible.

Any plants inside the enclosure must be free of pesticides and other chemicals.

have built effective pens inside greenhouses. To be a suitable place for a bearded dragon pen, a greenhouse should have controls for monitoring and maintaining desired temperatures, including whitewash, opening panels, fans, and heaters. It should also have pipes run nearby for easy access to water.

Inexpensive alternatives to pens are large plastic enclosures, screened on all sides, that are sold in the reptile trade. They are ideal for allowing lizards to bask outdoors in sunlight (see Chapter 4 on heating and lighting); however, do not place these all-screen enclosures on concrete or asphalt. Because both of these surfaces absorb heat when exposed to sun, dragons may quickly overheat and die. In any outdoor situation, the dragon will need access to shade, water, and climbing areas.

Some new owners think that any outdoor exposure is beneficial, but this is not true. Keep in mind that if an adult bearded dragon's preferred basking temperature is 105°F (41°C), and your outdoor temperature is 70°F (21°C) and breezy, that dragon will be cold.

Watch your dragon for its reaction to the outdoor conditions. Always pay attention to your dragon's reaction. If your dragon is showing stress marks on its stomach, it's unhappy, and if its color is darkening, it may be trying to warm up. Don't just depend on an outdoor thermometer to tell you if it's warm or cool enough.

Bearded dragons can enjoy some supervised outdoor time in a safe environment.

SUBSTRATES

Because of the potential risks of sand impaction, some people choose to initially raise baby bearded dragons on newspaper instead of sand. However, there are better options.

- **No substrate:** Many breeders raise their babies on bare floors within plastic tubs or glass tanks. Advantages of bare floors include easy cleanup, easy stool monitoring, a lack of hiding places for crickets, a minimal risk of impaction, and less intensive overall maintenance. Bare-floor enclosures are easy to empty of landscape structures and can be moved outside for washing with a garden hose and disinfecting. A disadvantage is that a bare floor requires regular wiping. As the dragon grows larger and messier, the bare tank becomes unattractive and tedious to clean. With larger animals, the hard, smooth floor surface can also lead to overgrown nails (unless trimmed) and bent toes.

- **Newspaper:** This is the substrate most recommended for quarantine and treatment of sick animals. Newspaper is cheap, readily available, easy to replace, and well suited for examining feces. Many specialists recommend newspaper for initially raising babies because it allows monitoring of stools and eliminates any risks of impaction. The downsides are that newspaper is visually unattractive, and regular or daily replacement can be labor-intensive. If used with adult dragons on a long-term basis, there is a risk of overgrown nails and bent toes. If you are going to use newspaper, print-free newspaper is the best option and is readily sourced locally or online.

- **Sand:** There are many different types and colors of sand available. It is better to stay away from sand during the juvenile stage. Many breeders still use silica-based play sand, but scooping through sand to remove feces day after day leaves one thing at the very least: bacteria. Add in leftover bits of greens baking in the 100°F (38°C) basking area, and you get a bacteria-laden environment. And, let's face it: no matter what kind of sand you use, it will stick to greens, veggies, and feeder insects. Intestinal impaction from sand ingested in this way is likely to occur. Additionally, there are instances of a bearded dragon's eyes swelling from sand particles that have made their way in. If you must use sand, the least harmful is white Repti-Sand by Zoo Med. It will still stick to the greens somewhat, but because it is almost dust-free and the particles very fine, there should be no issues with the dragons' eyes swelling. Limit this sand to adult enclosures only. Logically, adults have larger intestines and thus a better chance of passing ingested particles.

- **Paper towels:** Paper towels make it easy to keep the enclosure clean. Paper towels are easy to remove and replace if you are looking for uneaten feeders. It is a semi-alternative to using no substrate, and it keeps the babies' environment very clean.
- **Reptile carpet:** You can use reptile carpet as long as you change and wash it daily. Select a light color that the dragon will not mistake for food. When bearded dragons are placed on dark carpets, they tend to dull in color; light gray seems to work well. Replace the carpet as soon as the carpet loops start to loosen because the dragon's nails can get snagged in the loops, and the dragon can do itself serious harm trying to get the entangled toe(s) free. Loss of toenails, or worse, can result.

Keeping It Clean

With a sand substrate, using a 3-ounce (89mL) paper cup is an easy way to scoop out fecal matter and the surrounding sand.

- **Sandy soil:** Mixes of sand and soil work well with bearded dragons in outdoor enclosures; in outdoor setups, natural soils make up the floors of most screen houses and greenhouses. As with sand-only substrates, spot cleaning is easy. Sandy soil must be replaced on a regular basis. A problem with soil is that it can make dragons' colors appear browner and less colorful over time. Dust is also a problem.

LANDSCAPING

Many new owners make the understandable error of not including climbing areas in their adult bearded dragons' enclosures. This not only limits the space available for the dragons' activity but also makes for dull displays.

Remember, in Australia, beardies are often seen on the tops of fenceposts and railings, and you can reproduce these perching sites in captivity for adult dragons. By adding large pieces of driftwood, cork bark, or imitation rocks, you're providing your dragon with raised areas that make ideal basking sites; most hobbyists design their enclosures so that an elevated area is located under the basking light.

The down side of driftwood and cork is that feeder insects can wedge themselves into the natural cracks and lines or underneath, where the dragon cannot find them. These materials can also be hard to disinfect. Use low, flat rock-replica shelves and ledges that are long enough for an adult dragon to stretch out on and are easy to clean.

Part of cage maintenance is keeping basking surfaces and hiding spots clean.

Toxic Plants

Some readily available plants, such as sago palms (*Cycas revoluta*), are highly toxic to bearded dragons as well as to other pets. Inexpensive and attractive, sago palms are usually sold at big-box stores and even grocery stores. Every part of this plant, including the seeds and root ball, are toxic to animals and children. According to the Burnt Hills Veterinary Hospital, the signs of illness first appear about twelve hours after ingestion and include gastrointestinal symptoms, such as vomiting, diarrhea, and lethargy. The toxins in the plant cause severe liver failure with progressive weakness, jaundice, bruising, and bleeding, leading to death. It is estimated that 75-80 percent of animals that ingest this plant will die in spite of aggressive medical treatment.

If you have one of these plants in your home, keep it away from pets and children, preferably by disposing of it safely in a covered trash can or "rehoming" it with someone who does not have pets or young children. If you must have live plants, choose carefully.

Provide at least one raised site per enclosure, and maintain at least two-thirds of the floor surface as open space. Adult bearded dragons also enjoy shelters for sleeping at night or for brumation (shutting down) during the winter rest period. You can add suitable shelters when the time for brumation is approaching.

PLANTS

Popular vivarium plants, such as pothos or Chinese evergreen, become quickly crushed, nipped, trashed, and dried out in a bearded dragon setup, and only a few plant species are tough enough to hold up to bearded dragon abuse indoors. Better choices are ponytail palms (*Beaucarnea recurvata*) and snake plants (*Sansevieria* spp.), particularly the tougher ones with thick or cylindrical leaves that are better adapted to arid conditions.

With indoor setups, it is better to place plants in pots buried in the substrate rather than planting them directly into the substrate. This makes watering possible without wetting the entire setup and helps reduce water loss to the surrounding substrate. It also allows easy removal and replacement of plants as needed.

If your beardie is still trashing the plants, but you like the look of greenery, try artificial plants. They're less work, and your dragon shouldn't be tempted to eat them.

Nail Care

In captivity, if lizards are kept on solid surfaces or soft substrates, they can end up with overgrown nails and digits that bend to the side. Consider adding flat sections of rough rock, such as limestone, to your enclosure's landscaping because lizards wear down their nails by running or climbing on rock surfaces. If your beardie is not wearing down his nails enough on his own, trimming his nails regularly is the best alternative.

Make sure that any plants in the enclosure are safe for your dragons.

An elaborate setup requires more work to maintain and can cause a dragon, especially a young dragon, stress.

ENCLOSURE MAINTENANCE

It is important to monitor your bearded dragon daily to evaluate its attitude, condition, and health and to make sure that the enclosure is meeting your dragon's needs. Bearded dragons are active lizards that eat large amounts of food and consequently defecate correspondingly large amounts. In short, they tend to be messy. For this reason, regularly maintaining the enclosure is a must. With adult dragons, this means regularly scooping fecal material from the substrate or, better yet, using a substrate that can be frequently changed, such as print-free newspaper or paper towels, which should be changed every day.

In addition, if you keep water in the enclosure, you should replace it at least every day—more frequently if the dragons soil the water or the container. Wash and disinfect the water container regularly with a 1:10 bleach-to-water solution (using regular-strength bleach) to remove accumulating bacterial slime and traces of feces; rinse thoroughly after washing.

Remove dirty landscape features, such as rocks or driftwood, and disinfect them by soaking for a couple of hours in a container with a 1:10 solution of regular-strength bleach to water. Rinse them well to get rid of all traces of bleach before replacing them in the enclosure.

A Note on Bleach
Check to see if you are using concentrated bleach; it is three times as strong as regular bleach. Adjust the solution accordingly by adding 1 part bleach to 30 parts water.

Basic Setup for Hatchling to Large Juveniles

- 20-gallon (76L) long aquarium or terrarium tank
- Fluorescent tube-type fixture for the UVB tube
- UVB tube
- Clamp light fixture: Silver dome-type fixture rated for the wattage of your basking bulb
- Basking light: 60- and 75-watt clear basking bulbs; can be an incandescent replacement, such as a halogen
- Short, small, basking rock
- Water dish: Long, resin, molded rock-type dish, long enough for the dragon to lie down in
- Repti Calcium (or other brand) calcium supplement with vitamin D_3
- Herptivite® (or other brand) vitamin supplement

CHAPTER 4

THE IMPORTANCE OF HEATING AND LIGHTING

Providing proper heating and lighting is essential to keeping caged bearded dragons healthy. The dragons' activity and metabolic processes depend on proper light and heat gradients. Without them, your dragons will not survive.

HEATING

Providing adequate heat is critical to the welfare of bearded dragons, and there should be a 20°F (11°C) gradient between the top of the basking rock and the cool side floor. The primary source of heat should be a clear (not red) incandescent bulb or spotlight in a reflector-type fixture (clamp light) capable of handling the wattage and heat output. A fixture with a ceramic base and no electrical switch in the base typically lasts longer for this kind of use. Look for a fixture with a switch on the cord or plug the fixture into a surge-protector unit and use that switch to turn it on and off. Clamp the fixture to the short side of the tank over the basking site.

Watch your dragon's basking behavior to provide its preferred temperature.

For juveniles, 95 to 100°F (35 to 38°C) is a good place to start for the basking-site temperature, with the cool side floor at 75 to 80°F (24 to 27°C). You may find that your dragons like to bask at different temperatures, and you can achieve flexibility by trying different bulbs of different wattages, such as 60 watts and 75 watts, to see which bulb results in the desired temperatures. Another option is to plug the fixture into a light dimmer, which will allow you to adjust the heat output.

To determine the correct temperature for your bearded dragon, watch its basking behavior. If the dragon is happy at a certain temperature, he will be brightly colored and standing erect on, not next to, the basking rock. If he stands near the basking site, it is likely too hot. In this case, lower the heat by 5°F (about 3°C) and see how your bearded dragon reacts.

Some adults like it hotter. If your beardie spends all day on the basking rock, it may be too cool for him. Try raising the temperature at the basking site to 105°F (41°C) and see what happens. If his color is brighter, he looks more alert in his stance, and he tends to move over the enclosure at various times of the day, you have it right.

Placing a heat-absorbing landscape material under the basking light can help heat up a basking site more effectively. The problem is that the site can overheat, too. Artificial rocks made from molded resin work very well. Never use a "hot rock" because bearded dragons have sensitive stomachs that can be burned.

If you live in a very cold area, you might need supplemental heating at night. If the room where your bearded dragon's enclosure is falls below 68°F (20°C) at night, ceramic heating elements (that produce no light) can supply the additional heat needed to bring the tank or enclosure temperature up to 68 to 70°F (20 to 21°C), but no higher than that. Bearded dragons need a nighttime drop in temperature to cool down, but if the temperature inside the enclosure falls below 68°F (20°C), your dragon runs the risk of contracting a respiratory infection.

Beware of Fire Hazards!

Basking lights generate a great deal of heat and can start a fire if placed too close to combustible materials, such as curtains. It is very important to mount light fixtures securely to the top side of an enclosure and away from curtains and other flammable materials. If you have small children, cats, or other uncaged pets who are likely to topple fixtures or trip on electrical cords, limit their access to the room where you keep your bearded dragons.

Another fire hazard is placing lights on rugs or furniture while doing maintenance. This is especially dangerous when you have a light connected to a timer. Even though the light may be off when you move the fixture, the light will burn whatever lies beneath it when the timer turns the light on.

Finally, and most important, put a functioning smoke alarm in any room where heating lights or other kinds of heating units are used for reptiles.

UNDERSTANDING HEAT

A key to successfully keeping reptiles is understanding the role of heat. Bearded dragons are ectotherms, which means that they depend on environmental temperatures to achieve and maintain optimal body temperatures. However, bearded dragons are not passive in their relationship with environmental temperatures. They adjust their body temperatures with various behaviors, including selection of thermal zones. For example, after a cool night in the desert, a lizard may crawl out into sunlight at midmorning, flatten its body, and adopt an overall darker coloration to increase heat absorption so that it can quickly warm up to an effective operating temperature, which allows it to be alert and act quickly.

Once it reaches an optimal temperature, the lizard may hunt insects, perform displays for other lizards, and be watchful for potential predators. However, as the midday sun causes air and surface temperatures to rise even higher, the lizard may begin to overheat and will move out of the sun to rest in shade or under

A cool spot, around 20°F (11°C) cooler than the basking area, is essential in a dragon's enclosure.

shelter until the temperature cools down. This is known as *thermoregulation*, and it is a critical aspect for caring for our dragons in indoor enclosures. As mentioned, the bearded dragon needs to be able to move from the basking spot to a cooler zone that is 20°F (11°C) cooler than the basking spot. In this way, the dragon regulates its internal body temperature as necessary. Heating up under the basking light will stimulate hunger and allow for digestion of food and calcium supplements. Moving to the cool side of the enclosure allows the dragon to cool down, lowering its internal body temperature.

Light goes hand-in-hand with heat in providing an optimal bearded dragon environment.

One of the interesting features of reptiles is that that they heat up quickly and cool down relatively slowly. In fact, one of the studies showing this was done with the Eastern bearded dragon (Bartholomew and Tucker, 1963). Individuals with a 68°F (20°C) body temperature placed in a 103°F (39°C) chamber heated up to 101°F (38°C) in about thirty-eight minutes but, under reverse conditions, required more than fifty minutes to cool from 103 to 68°F (39 to 20°C). Thus, a heated reptile can store heat and maintain a relatively high body temperature for an extended period of time.

Optimal temperatures allow efficient metabolism and immune-system activity in bearded dragons. If a dragon is kept too cool, its metabolic processes will occur at a slower rate, and the immune system will become depressed. Cool temperatures reduce the digestion rate, too, which can lead to gastrointestinal problems, such as decomposition of food in the gut and bloating. The equilibria of bacteria and protozoa in the gut may also be thrown out of balance. Moreover, the rate of clearing uric acid and other compounds through the kidneys is reduced at suboptimal temperatures, and the risks of kidney disease increased. Growth rate, which depends on appetite, rapid digestion, and effective metabolism, is directly affected by temperature. Therefore, keeping a bearded dragon at the correct basking and cool-side temperatures results in a bright, healthy animal. Incorrect temperatures or an incorrect temperature gradient will result in sickness and ultimately death.

LIGHTING

Good lighting is critical to the health of bearded dragons. Without it, they are less spirited, less active, and dull in color. Even the moods of humans are affected by low light exposure. How could one expect a sun-loving animal from Australia (which is an extremely bright continent) to thrive under low light conditions? You may have seen bearded dragons in pet stores kept under low light conditions, with only a ceramic infrared heater as the primary source of heat. In addition to incandescent-type lights as heat and light sources for basking, bearded dragons need full-spectrum or high-UVB reptile bulbs provided overhead in fluorescent fixtures that run the length of the enclosure. There are new compact fluorescent-type UVB bulbs on the market; however, the long-tube fluorescent-type UVB bulbs produce far more visual light than compact screw-in types.

If possible, locate your dragon in a bright, well-lit room of the house. When bearded dragons are kept in a very bright environment, they eat better, are brighter in color, and are much more active than without bright light.

Mercury Vapor Bulb Caution

If you use a mercury vapor bulb for an adult in a large tank or enclosure, make sure that the bulb is at one end of the tank so the dragon can move away at will. Mercury vapor bulbs for babies kept indoors in 20-gallon (76L) long tanks are not recommended. Baby bearded dragons under mercury vapor bulbs have been killed within twenty-four hours. More UVB is not always better!

Providing UVB is critical to aiding the dragon in generating vitamins and minerals. It is hypothesized that basking lizards, such as bearded dragons, manufacture vitamin D_3 when exposed to UVB radiation from sunlight. Because lizards need vitamin D_3 to effectively absorb calcium, a lack of this vitamin in the diet or a lack of exposure to a UVB source can lead to calcium deficiency in the dragon. This condition becomes very noticeable in baby lizards, which require large amounts of calcium to build their rapidly growing skeletons.

A calcium deficiency in bearded dragons further results in metabolic bone disease (MBD), a crippling disease that deforms the bones, especially those in the back. To prevent MBD, provide appropriate amounts of calcium and vitamin D_3 in your dragon's diet along with exposure to UVB radiation in the form of sunlight or UVB-generating bulbs or fluorescent-type tubes.

Bearded dragons do, in fact, eat more, grow faster, and remain healthier and more active when provided with sunlight or full-spectrum/reptile UVB fluorescent tubes. In one experiment, specimens that were fed *ad libitum* grew from hatchling to 14 inches (36cm) long in fourteen weeks by combining a spotlight heat source with full-spectrum bulbs placed 6 inches (15cm) above the experimental group. This group's growth rate was significantly greater compared to specimens raised under conditions where any of three factors—light-generated heat, UVB-generating light, and food availability—were limited.

Mercury vapor bulbs sold in the reptile trade fit incandescent fixtures, produce good levels of UVB, and emit heat. They are effective as a UVB source; however, you must ensure that your dragon does not become dehydrated in an enclosure with a mercury vapor bulb. Do not use them with juvenile bearded dragons because the results are usually disastrous. There are also bulbs, such as Mega-Ray® bulbs, that produce very little to no heat but do provide UVB. If you use this product, make sure to give your dragon a basking lamp for heat and also some sort of visual lighting.

One easy way to provide UVB is to expose lizards to sunlight. The safest way to expose them to sunlight is to use a screen-sided "basking cage," which reduces the risks of overheating. A commonly used alternative is to place the bearded dragons in a large opaque or white plastic storage container with a screen top. Glass-sided, clear, or bare-floor plastic containers risk overheating and are often lethal to dragons when placed in the sun. Instead, use sand and cover part of the storage container with cardboard for shade. Even with screen-sided enclosures, you should always provide an area of shade so your bearded dragon can get out of the sun. Placement of basking cages is also important: grass and soil are safe, but beware of concrete patios or asphalt surfaces, which build up heat in the sun and can kill your dragon.

LIGHT, HEAT, AND COLORATION

Proper light and heat can help bring out your bearded dragon's true colors. The bright orange-reds and yellows of certain lines of bearded dragon do not become fully expressed if temperatures are not optimal for that dragon. One or more factors related to light (and possibly heat) appear necessary to trigger the hyperxanthic response, which is an increase in yellow and orange skin pigments. This is comparable to the hypermelanistic response in humans, which is the increase of the dark pigment melanin when human skin is exposed to UV radiation from the sun. Bearded dragons raised outdoors under greenhouse plastic that filters out most of the UV radiation become just as bright as individuals kept in the open, so UV radiation may not necessarily be the triggering factor.

Many bearded dragons are brightest under correct basking temperatures, very bright visual light, and ReptiSun 10.0 fluorescent UVB tubes or Arcadia T-8s.

Various types of tanks, including glass tanks, top cages in various colors, wooden enclosures in various stains, all-screen cages, and enclosures with solid sides and backs can all affect coloration. Bright beardies placed in dark-stained or granite-colored enclosures darkened immediately, even with optimal basking temperature and UVB output. In screen cages, brilliant-colored dragons dulled. They were cold, and the screen blocked the visual light from the room.

Conversely, the dragons placed in all-white melamine enclosures with solid tops, sides, and backs with sliding glass doors in front were brightest in color when compared to all of the other caging systems. This makes sense because, as previously mentioned, Australia is a very bright continent!

Lighting helps keep a dragon's colors rich and vivid.

BRUMATION (WINTER SHUTDOWN)

Once mature (after one year of age), bearded dragons usually enter a state of shutdown, commonly termed "brumation," in which they remain relatively inactive, hidden in shelters or lying on the ground and eating little, if at all. If raised under indoor conditions, babies hatched out in the summer won't undergo winter shutdown until the following year (at about eighteen months of age). During brumation, dragons must be maintained at cooler temperatures (60 to 70°F [16 to 21°C]), something easily achieved in most homes by placing the enclosure on the floor of a room during the winter months. Owners should

UVB Output

Keep in mind that a bulb's UVB does not last forever. At some point, the UVB output will fall below the therapeutic range that your bearded dragon needs. The bulb will still produce light, but with no UVB. Heat causes UVB to dissipate faster, which is why you will notice that the end of a fluorescent-type UVB bulb turns black at the end next to the basking light. One way to extend the life of a UVB tube is to flip the tube end to end every few months. It also makes sense to invest in a UVB meter to measure the tube's UVB output. Change UVB bulbs when the readings drop below 70 percent of the initial burn-in, or about every six months.

Bright light and heat during the day is balanced by "lights out" overnight.

decrease the wattage of basking lights to reduce the basking site's temperature to 75 to 80°F (24 to 27°C), and leave the basking lights on for only eight to ten hours daily. Many owners are alarmed by their dragons' drastic change in behavior during brumation and worry that their dragons may be sick. A period of brumation, however, is normal for this species. Brumation can last from a few weeks to five months. If bearded dragons are healthy, they will lose little or no weight during this period and will remain in good condition, showing no signs of disease (e.g., sunken eyes, gaping, twitching, wheezing).

There are two approaches that beardie owners can take during brumation. In the first approach, the owner can create a shutdown cycle of cooler temperatures and shorter day length, similar to what happens in the wild. The owner needs to reduce, and then eliminate, the dragon's food about one week before the onset of cooler temperatures, allowing the dragon to empty any remaining fecal matter in its intestines. Alternatively, in the second approach, an owner can wait, observe the dragon closely, and then create brumation conditions as soon as the dragon shows signs of reduced activity and food intake.

The end of brumation is marked by a shift in behavior following the increase in heat and light that accompanies spring. At this point, the owner should return the dragon to normal conditions as soon as it starts basking and feeding again. Start with easily digestible foods, such as greens, until the dragon's normal bodily functions return. Soaking daily will help the dragon wake up.

CHAPTER 5

DIET AND FEEDING MANAGEMENT

Bearded dragons consume a wide variety of animal and plant foods throughout their lives. Studies of the stomach contents of wild bearded dragons in Australia showed that, when young, these lizards eat about 50 percent live food and 50 percent plants; when mature, they eat mostly 65–90 percent plant matter. Observations of thousands of dragons in breeding facilities suggest that they have similar food preferences when living in certain conditions in captivity. However, under indoor conditions, juveniles will consume more live, moving prey when they are young (approximately 90 percent live prey and 10 percent plant matter). Bearded dragons eat

Insects make up a large part of a pet bearded dragon's daily diet.

more vegetarian fare as they reach subadulthood to adulthood. The wild diet of bearded dragon juveniles differs perhaps due to the abundant variety of wild prey. Indoors, the commercially available prey items may not be as nutritionally dense, which could be why babies will consume more live prey indoors than in the wild. Young bearded dragons need a variety of prey, so provide two or three different types, such as crickets, Dubia roaches, and black soldier fly larvae, to provide nutritional variety.

Very young bearded dragons really do need live prey. Without live food, there is a high risk of stunted growth, malnutrition, and even death from starvation. Moreover, baby dragons housed together will cannibalize each other, nipping off toes and tail tips if hungry and deprived of adequate amounts of live prey. If you want a bearded dragon as a pet but won't accept crickets in the house, feed black soldier fly larvae (such as Phoenix Worms). These high-calcium, extremely nutritious worms make no noise, require no feeding, and need only be kept in a cup at room temperature. You can also feed silkworms and/or green hornworms, which need to be fed but not refrigerated. You should not feed green hornworms to your bearded dragon exclusively, or even every day, because they are very high in fat. Mature dragons can stay alive for some time without live prey, but they will be unhappy and will not thrive.

The enthusiastic and eclectic appetites of bearded dragons give owners an opportunity to interact with their pets and bring much enjoyment to both species. Food treats can be used as rewards and to attract the attention of a pet dragon. Many a dragon happily bounds up to an owner when snacks are in hand, and food often serves as the strongest bond between dragon and owner. Beardies are nutritionally robust, handling many food treats and careful diet changes with minimal or easily resolved digestive disturbance. Sound diets for bearded dragons have built-in nutritional flexibility that allows for treats and snacks without risking imbalances. In other words, bearded dragons can consume a wide variety of foods as long as those foods are appropriate.

FOOD AND SUPPLEMENT SOURCES
INSECTS

Bearded dragons are usually fed commercially bred invertebrates, such as crickets (*Acheta domestica*), Dubia roaches (*Blaptica dubia*), superworms (*Zophobus morio*), waxworms (*Galleria mellonella*), black soldier fly larvae (*Hermetia illucens*), and others, which are available for sale online and in many pet-supply shops. You should avoid mealworms because they can cause intestinal impaction and metabolic bone disease due to their high phosphorus content. Bearded dragons cannot be maintained well on flying

Salads and other fresh produce provide both nutrients and water.

insects, such as houseflies, which easily evade the dragons. Although some dragons may eat earthworms and other garden worms, these are not typical prey for the species, thus most will not eat them.

VERTEBRATE PREY

Larger bearded dragons do not hesitate to eat small lizards and, in fact, appear to relish them. In captivity, adults also feed on juvenile (pink to fuzzy) mice, which can be a useful part of a varied diet for larger dragons, providing nutrients such as calcium as well as many vitamins and trace minerals that are not readily available from invertebrates and salads. Vertebrate prey requires you to feed them balanced diets and water if you keep them for more than a day. Feeding your dragons frozen or thawed pinkies and fuzzy mice is a humane and convenient option.

GREENS AND OTHER PRODUCE

Regarding vegetarian foods, torn dark leafy greens are best for juvenile dragons, while subadult and adult bearded dragons can make use of a variety of approved vegetables and fruits. You can also feed your dragons plants from fields and lawns that haven't been treated with pesticides and herbicides; they especially relish leaves and blossoms from clover, dandelion, and mustard. Other treats include petals from rose blossoms, hibiscus, and calendula (again, untreated with chemicals). Calendula is very easy to grow from seed and has beautiful yellow flowers.

Did You Know?

If you plan to feed pinkie mice to your adult bearded dragons, consider that mice can raise cholesterol to an unhealthy level if fed too frequently. It's better to stick with insects and worms as feeders.

PELLETS

Commercial diets for bearded dragons are primarily in the form of dry pellets, marketed either specifically for bearded dragons or for other pets. No bearded dragon's diet should consist solely of dry commercial foods, whether bearded dragon food or food made for other animals. Use dry food in an emergency, but otherwise stick to live food and fresh vegetables, greens, and fruits. The advantages and drawbacks of commercial diets are discussed later in this chapter.

SUPPLEMENTS

Bearded dragons require supplementation with a powdered vitamin/mineral supplement and calcium to make up for the deficiencies and high phosphorus levels found in commercially produced insects and produce. Reptile supplements are readily available online and in stores that sell reptile supplies. Because supplements vary widely in their formulations, you should carefully examine their labels to determine their ingredients. Ideally, you should select a source of calcium, such as calcium carbonate powder, plus a supplement that contains vitamins and minerals, including trace minerals. You need to give your dragons only small amounts—just enough to lightly coat, or dust, the insects.

Most diets for bearded dragons require nutrient supplementation because few of the foods in their diets are nutritionally complete or balanced. Invertebrates (crickets, Dubia roaches, superworms, waxworms) lack enough calcium because they have no skeletons and are deficient in several vitamins and trace minerals. Vegetarian foods (such as greens, carrots, bananas, etc.) are deficient in a variety of essential nutrients, such as calcium, and certain amino acids, fatty acids, and trace minerals.

Generally, baby bearded dragons require daily supplementation, and older animals need gradually decreasing rates of supplementation so that they are supplemented weekly or every other week. The type and amount of supplementation needed by your dragon depends on many factors. For example, dragons housed outdoors with access to the ground obtain the vitamin D_3 from basking in the sun and many trace minerals from access to soil, whereas those kept indoors would need these essential nutrients provided in their diet.

Supplemental Calcium

Calcium is critical for healthy bone growth in bearded dragons. You'll want to feed your dragons foods high in calcium, but dragons need supplemental calcium as well, regardless of diet.

Most supplements emphasizing vitamins and minerals fail to provide enough calcium to meet the needs of dragons. Thus, two types of supplements are often necessary: one containing vitamins and minerals (including a little calcium) and the other containing mainly calcium (such as calcium carbonate, bonemeal, and cuttlebone).

Dragons needing the most calcium are babies and egg-laying females. Appropriate rates of supplementation vary with the dragon's age and size, housing (indoors or out), calorie intake, amount of calcium provided by the diet, and amounts of several other nutrients in the diet, including phosphorus and vitamin D_3. Generally, baby dragons are supplemented with calcium daily, and rates decrease with age and size.

Bearded dragons require 1–1.5 percent of the diet's dry matter as calcium, and about 0.5–0.9 percent phosphorus. Attention is often given to the ratio of calcium to phosphorus in the diet. It should be in the range of 1:1 to 2:1 calcium:phosphorus (Ca:P). However, the amounts of dietary calcium and phosphorus are more important than the ratio. For example, if a diet contained only 0.4 percent calcium and 0.2 percent phosphorus, the Ca:P ratio would be 2:1, but the amounts would be deficient, and a dragon fed this diet would develop calcium deficiency.

Of the commonly available calcium supplements, calcium content is 40 percent in calcium carbonate, 38 percent in limestone, 18 percent in calcium lactate, and 9 percent in calcium gluconate. Calcium and phosphorus contents are 24 percent and 12 percent in bonemeal, and 24 percent and 18 percent in dicalcium phosphate.

Supplemental Vitamin D

Bearded dragons require vitamin D for a variety of functions, including the formation of strong bones by aiding the absorption of dietary calcium. Dietary vitamin D comes in two forms—vitamin D_2 (ergocaciferol), which occurs in plants, and vitamin D_3 (cholecalciferol), which occurs in animal tissue, especially liver. There is evidence that reptiles cannot utilize vitamin D_2, so vitamin D_3 is always recommended for bearded dragons. Basking lizards such as bearded dragons can also make vitamin D_3 by exposing their skin to UVB light rays from the sun or from special UVB lamps.

Although some dragons seem to do well without dietary vitamin D if they live outdoors year-round, most bearded dragons who live all or part of the year indoors will need a source of dietary D_3. Vitamin D_3 is listed on food labels as cholecalciferol, animal sterol, D-activated animal sterol, irradiated animal sterol, or vitamin D_3. Don't assume that the term "vitamin D" in the label ingredient list is actually D_3, for it may be D_2 and unusable by your dragon.

As with many nutrients, vitamin D is toxic when fed in excess. Toxicity most commonly occurs from overzealous supplementation with vitamin/mineral products. There is no need to thickly coat crickets

In the wild, bearded dragons get enough vitamin D from the sun.

Managing Prey

Feed crickets, roaches, superworms, and other prey no later than two hours before lights out. A bearded dragon needs time to digest food under the basking light. Food that sits in the gut undigested can cause all sorts of issues, and uneaten prey that is roaming at night can stress your dragon or even bite its toes, tail, and face. Roaming hungry crickets have been known to fatally wound baby dragons. Always remove uneaten prey items (except black soldier fly larvae or butterworms) within thirty minutes to one hour of feeding.

until they are white, for example, three times a day. Toxicity also occurs from the ingestion of certain types of rat and mouse poisons. Signs of toxicity often involve multiple organ systems because of widespread soft-tissue calcification.

The active form of vitamin D is made by a series of chemical transformations in the liver and then the kidneys. Thus, diseases of the liver or kidneys will affect vitamin D metabolism and can lead to signs of deficiency or toxicity. Disorders caused by too little or too much vitamin D, or diseases of the liver and kidneys, which lead to secondary problems with vitamin D, require veterinary attention.

WATER

Water is the most important element for a bearded dragon's health. Long-term dehydration causes renal (kidney) failure. Kidney failure causes death and has taken many bearded dragons before their time.

Keep in mind that although bearded dragons come from an arid climate, they now live in your home. How well they thrive is dependent on adequate water, high-quality food, and correct lighting and temperatures. The following information will help you keep your bearded dragons well hydrated, healthy, and happy.

Offer your dragon high-quality, clean, contaminant-free water. Generally, water that is safe for you is safe for your bearded dragon. Offer clean water at least once a day. The water bowl should be long enough for the dragon to fully lie down in (about 8 inches [20cm] long for a juvenile), and the water level should only be as high as its elbows. For an adult dragon, the water container should also be long enough for the dragon to stretch out its entire body, but with a shoulder-high water level. The water must be visible to the dragon when the dragon is up on all fours. Spraying the sides of the habitat with water may prove particularly useful for watering hatchling babies who, as a rule, don't readily recognize standing water.

One common mistake for new owners is buying a small, shallow water dish, thinking that the dragon will lower his head into it to drink. This is not the case. The main purpose of a water dish is to allow a bearded dragon to soak, and bearded dragons enter their water dishes often for this purpose. In fact, some bearded dragons are regular water babies!

In addition to the water dish, misting is critical for dragons indoors and in enclosures. When raising dragons indoors, some breeders recommend misting adults and babies twice a day, using hot tap water in the morning and warm tap water in the evening, just before lights out. Misting the glass as well creates a slight film when it dries that will block your dragon's reflection if it lives in a glass tank.

Once the dragon reaches the large subadult or adult stage, soak it in a pan of shoulder-high water, two or three times a week, for about ten minutes at a time. To ensure that your adult bearded dragon gets enough water, a good backup method is to manually give it water with a plastic dripper bottle, slowly squeezing the bottle so that droplets of water fall at the tip of your dragon's snout. Sometimes, a large water dish in the habitat can raise the humidity. If that's the case, you'll need to soak your beardie every day and make sure droplets fall on the tip of its snout to encourage it to drink.

Bearded dragons also obtain some water through their diet; many of the foods recommended for dragons, such as invertebrates and salads, contain water. Insects contain about 60 percent water, depending on the insect; for example, hornworms and silkworms are quite a bit higher in water content.

Daily exposure to water is likely unnecessary under certain specific husbandry systems if dragons are kept outdoors. However, for bearded dragons maintained indoors, especially

Dirty Water

Most problems with water quality arise from a dragon fouling its water with feces or decomposing food; therefore, be sure to keep an eye on your dragon's water receptacle and clean it as soon as you notice that the water is soiled.

Avoid Dehydration

A dehydrated dragon will have wrinkles on the sides of his body, a sleepy-eyed look, and slime threads running from the top to the bottom of his mouth when his mouth is open. One emergency-care method is to "plump" Phoenix Worms in water until they start wriggling around and then drain the water and place the worms in the dragons' feeding bowl.

You'll also need to make some adjustments to your husbandry techniques. Make sure that you are properly misting juveniles or misting/soaking adults and offering high-quality fresh greens daily to dragons of any age. Recheck your temperatures to make sure that the basking and cool sides of the tank or enclosure are not too hot. Many times, owners will set up their dragons' living areas perfectly but forget to make necessary adjustments. For example, when summer rolls around and the air-conditioner is on, your dragon will need a higher-wattage basking lamp. Conversely, in winter, with the heater blowing, your dragon may need a lower-wattage bulb to compensate.

those in heated homes or in dry climates, giving them access to a water dish and misting, as well as supplemental soaking for adults, is a must.

HOW MUCH TO FEED AND SUPPLEMENT

As a general rule, feed a bearded dragon as many crickets as it can consume in a thirty-minute feeding. If you keep black soldier fly larvae in a bowl all day, feed as many as the dragon will eat in a day. Adult dragons can be maintained with constant access to invertebrates (during the day) if the prey are confined to a bowl and not free-roaming and creating stress for the dragons. Also make greens available in the enclosure during the day, removing any foods that might decompose at night.

Add supplements carefully to insects, providing just a light coating. An easy way to do this is by placing calcium supplements in a salt shaker and the vitamin supplements in a pepper shaker. Make sure you label the shakers so you know which

is which. As for the size of live prey, bearded dragons almost never suffer from eating prey that are too small, though some may not eat them. Bearded dragons can be picky about the exact size of the crickets they will eat. But many dragons, especially babies, have died from eating prey that are too large. A general guideline is to feed crickets that are no longer than the width between the dragon's eyes. For babies, that means feeding crickets that are just a week or two old and no more than ¼ inch (6mm). For juveniles, ⅜-inch (1cm) crickets are prime choice. Older juveniles can graduate to ½-inch (1.3cm) crickets and so on. As a rule of thumb, move the dragons up one size when they are consistently eating more than 50 crickets a day, every day. As your dragon grows, you can feed it other prey, but always follow the rule that the prey should be no longer than the width between the dragon's eyes.

Some dragons relish hard-shelled beetles. May beetles and June bugs have been given as treats for adults in early summer. There is a risk in feeding wild foods, though, as many insecticides have a slow-kill formula, so there is no way to know if beetles have been exposed to poison. For this reason and others, it's best to stay away from wild prey.

FEEDING GUIDELINES: AN AGE-BY-AGE GUIDE
BABIES

Newly hatched bearded dragons may take a day or two to begin eating. During this time, the baby receives needed nutrition from its own reserves, mostly through its reabsorbed yolk sac. After a day or two, though, a baby dragon should be a lively feeder, so observe it to make sure it is eating. The hatchling bearded dragon must be able to find the food and water in its enclosure.

Once a baby starts eating, it should be a lively feeder.

Homegrown Foods

Some specialty foods, such as arugula, that are very beneficial for bearded dragons may be hard to find in some areas. However, if you are so inclined, you can grow your own from seeds relatively easily. For example, certain types of greens as well as kabocha squash grow particularly well in very large pots.

Babies should be started on one- to two-week-old crickets and graduated to larger crickets as they grow older. Offer the baby dragon only a few live, small (about ¼-inch [6mm]) crickets, Dubia roaches, or black soldier fly larvae. To determine appropriate cricket size, remember that the crickets' length should be no greater than the width between the dragon's eyes. At the hatchling stage, offering a larger number of smaller prey promotes more efficient digestion than offering a smaller number of larger prey. Pinhead crickets, however, are too small to be of benefit, and the dragon may not eat them, choosing to starve.

Don't overload the tank with crickets, which will stress the dragon. Loose crickets will crawl over the lizard and may bite it. Feed one at a time, watching to see how the dragon reacts. If he runs right after and consumes the first cricket, give it another. If the dragon does not chase the cricket immediately, the dragon may be afraid of you. In this case, throw five crickets, one at a time, against the far wall under the heat lamp. The crickets will bounce, and the movement will attract the baby's attention.

Leave, come back after thirty minutes, and remove any uneaten crickets. Keep track of when and how many your dragon consumes. If it has eaten all five crickets, give it eight crickets at the next feeding, and so on. Offer only as many crickets as your dragon will eat within thirty minutes. In this way, you get to know the feeding habits of your dragon, and the dragon will not be overwhelmed by crickets running all over it. Offer crickets two to three times daily.

Provide water in the resin-type molded water dishes meant for this purpose. Very young hatchlings are often thirsty, so misting twice daily—first thing in the morning with hot tap water and last thing at night with warm tap water before lights out—will help them drink.

For babies who are having trouble drinking, lightly misting the walls and the furnishings inside the enclosure can help. Your goal is to provide drinking water for the hatchlings, not to create a super-humid environment or standing puddles of water. This is why paper towels make a good substrate for a baby beardie's enclosure—if the bottom of the enclosure gets soaked, it is easy to swap out the wet paper towels for dry.

Once a day, dust crickets with a mixture of powdered calcium carbonate and a vitamin-mineral supplement. One way to do this is to place an allotment of crickets in a smooth-sided container from

which they can't escape, such as a glass jar or small plastic pitcher, and then adding an amount of supplement appropriate to the number of crickets. As a rule of thumb, a small pinch of supplement will be adequate to coat the insects for feeding one to three baby dragons. Gently swirl the container for a few seconds until the crickets are lightly coated with the supplement and then feed the crickets to your hungry dragon. As mentioned, another way to coat the crickets is with salt and pepper shakers: put the calcium supplement in one and the vitamin/mineral supplement in the other and then label both shakers. It is very easy to shake out the supplements needed into the glass jar with the crickets for feeding. If you find crickets too smelly and noisy, and you want to feed Dubia roaches instead, one roach equals four to six crickets and offers more meat than the equivalent number of crickets.

It helps to introduce new foods when lizards are young and inquisitive. Offer finely chopped or torn greens—whatever the babies prefer—daily (inverted plastic tops from containers work well as food trays), and leave them in the enclosure throughout the day. The baby dragons will run through the food and often ignore it initially. As the days pass, however, the dragons will nibble on these foods and begin to include them as part of their daily intake. Remove uneaten greens at the end of each day.

Do not offer treats or snacks to very young dragons. These lizards are growing rapidly and need to fill up on highly nutritious supplemented crickets or other high-quality prey if they are to achieve their genetic potential for size, conformation, and vigor. The dragons are actually less interested in snacks during this phase. The focus of the baby dragons should also be the focus of the owner—the availability

No Force-Feeding

During brumation (winter shutdown), adult bearded dragons are inactive and may not feed at all. Do not force-feed them at this time. Once your dragons are active again, return to the usual feeding schedule.

of enough well-supplemented crickets or other prey items in a hospitable, wholesome environment to allow for optimal development.

Common feeding problems at this stage include starvation and malnutrition. Starvation is characterized by poor growth, loss of weight, and often death. It is due to poor food intake arising from a variety of causes, including temperatures too cool and/or lighting too dim, which will inhibit the feeding response; inappropriate foods, such

A dim enclosure will not stimulate appetite and digestion.

as greens only, commercial pellets only, or crickets of the wrong size; and large, rapidly growing dragons that may be bullying slower-growing dragons, reducing food intake in the runts.

A secondary problem from inadequate food intake is mutilation. Hungry baby dragons will nip the toes and tail tips of other dragons. If you observe this, add another daily meal or increase the amount of crickets fed at each meal. Or, better yet, separate the babies, keeping aggressive dragons away from those lower on the social hierarchy.

Malnutrition occurs from feeding imbalanced diets, such as unsupplemented crickets or only mealworms. Calcium deficiency is common, arising from deficiencies of dietary calcium and/or dietary vitamin D_3 or UVB. Young dragons with symptoms of calcium deficiency (shaking, twitching, paralysis, or lameness) need veterinary treatment and diet evaluation.

Did You Know?
Bearded dragons enjoy waxworms, but many will refuse to eat other prey once they taste the fat in waxworms.

JUVENILES (TWO TO FOUR MONTHS)

During this stage, young bearded dragons are eating machines. They grow very rapidly, increasing their size more than 4,000 percent in their first six months under optimal conditions. Offer appropriately sized crickets twice daily—as many as the young dragon(s) will eat in 30 minutes—and supplement crickets once daily.

Offer salads of torn or finely chopped greens. When the dragons near four months of age, you can add some fresh green beans, shredded butternut squash, and tiny bits of kiwi, papaya, or melon once a week; no supplementation is needed for these occasional snacks. Remember that while dragons are in a fast growth stage, they need the nutrition from feeder insects more than from vegetables and fruit. When they are older, they will enjoy colorful chopped fruits and vegetables mixed into their greens.

Introduce other small invertebrates, such as Dubia roaches, black soldier fly larvae, silkworms, or small hornworms, for nutritional variety. The calcium content of black soldier fly larvae is very high, so if you are feeding only black soldier fly larvae,

Eat Your Greens!
The overall best greens are dark leafy greens, such as arugula, romaine, mustard greens, turnip greens, collards, dandelion greens, kale, spinach, and bagged mixed greens. Romaine is a plus because it is palatable, it is nutritious, and it contains moderate calcium (0.7 percent), beta-carotene (over 50 retinol equivalents per gram of dry matter), and fiber (35 percent). Romaine lettuce has been fed successfully to bearded dragons through all life stages. While some experts state that greens should be supplemented to provide missing essential nutrients, many beardies prefer greens without supplements and have never suffered any calcium deficiencies.

Commercially available locusts are popular with beardie fanciers in the UK.

the dragons will still need a vitamin/mineral supplement.

Common nutritional problems seen at this stage include inadequate feeding because the offered prey insects are too large for the dragon. Consumption of too-large crickets may also be associated with partial paralysis of the legs. Owners sometimes want to rush into larger crickets, but be patient. Pushing baby bearded dragons to their limit on prey size is risking problems.

High-Calcium Foods versus Poor Calcium Sources

As a general rule, you cannot feed large enough quantities of high-calcium foods to make up for the deficiencies of the calcium-deficient foods in a dragon's diet. Supplementation with calcium is almost always needed. Following is the calcium content of some popular greens and fruit for bearded dragons.

- Dandelion greens (1.3 percent)
- Mustard greens (1.3 percent)
- Spinach (1.1 percent)
- Kale (0.8 percent)
- Romaine (0.7 percent)
- Alfalfa sprouts (0.3 percent)
- Peas (0.1 percent)
- Melons (0.1 percent)
- Mango (0.06 percent)
- Apple (0.05 percent)
- Papaya (0.02 percent)
- Banana (0.02 percent)

Provide a greater variety of produce to your subadult dragon.

Calcium deficiency is often seen at this stage. Parasitic and infectious diseases may result from failure to keep food and water scrupulously clean. Juvenile bearded dragons are quite active, and they'll frequently scamper through food and water, soiling everything in their path. A part of feeding management is maintenance of hygienic conditions.

SUBADULT (FOUR MONTHS TO SEXUAL MATURITY)

In this stage of adolescence, offer crickets twice a day. As the dragon grows, gradually increase the size of crickets offered up to 1 inch (2.5cm). Remember to supplement the crickets once a day.

Subadult dragons enjoy smaller superworms, especially freshly shed white superworms, as well as juvenile Dubia roaches, young mice (both pink and fuzzy), black soldier fly larvae, other feeder roaches, silkworms, butterworms, and hornworms. These prey animals are enjoyed by most dragons and are conducive to but not essential for good health.

Dietary Cautions

Owners have occasionally used alfalfa hay or pellets as enclosure substrates for their dragons, but these substrates/foods are highly dangerous and should be avoided. If a dragon ingests this type of substrate, it risks intestinal blockage; also, these products mold readily in the presence of moisture (from spilled water, fresh salads, excretory products, and misted water), which risks digestive upsets and pneumonia if the dragon consumes or inhales mold spores.

When offering snacks and treats, keep in mind that too much of any one food can lead to diarrhea. Usually, digestive upsets are self-contained and resolve within a day. Occasionally, serious gastrointestinal disease and dehydration develop, necessitating veterinary treatment. Owners may be alarmed by a change in the color of their dragon's stool, but this often simply reflects the passage of pigments from vegetables, such as the orange carotenoids found in carrots.

Salads become a more substantial part of diet at this stage, so give more attention to their nutritional balance. You may start adding vegetables, such as fresh beans and other legumes (peas), green beans, okra, and squash, as well as fruits, including bananas, melons, apples, papayas, and berries, to the salads. Chop or tear all salad components into bite-sized pieces suited to the size of your dragon.

You can supplement the salad with a light sprinkling of calcium and vitamin/mineral supplement to improve its nutritional quality, but some dragons will not eat supplemented salad. In those cases, it is better for the dragon to eat unsupplemented greens than no greens at all.

ADULTS

Offer adult bearded dragons appropriately sized crickets and/or superworms daily or every second day, depending on the dragon. Other prey for adults can include Dubia roaches, black soldier fly larvae, silkworms, butterworms, hornworms, and waxworms. You may also offer treats, such as canned grasshoppers and crickets. At this stage, you may start to offer small vertebrates, such as young mice.

Offer supplemented salads daily. Bearded dragons can eat as much salad as they wish, as long as it is nutritionally balanced and complete. Feed a variety of greens along with pieces of higher-calcium fruits and vegetables. Feed snacks and treats that your dragon can swallow in one gulp once or twice daily.

If you have these flowers and leaves available, and you are sure that there are no pesticides on them, you can offer a rose, carnation, dahlia, daylily, dandelion, hibiscus, pansy, hollyhock, clover, maple leaf, or mulberry leaf—but only two or three times weekly.

Did You Know?

Adult dragons relish young lizards, so they should never be allowed access to pet baby dragons in the household. An adult bearded dragon will waste no time in eating a baby bearded dragon.

If you feed fruits, make sure they are fresh. A few dried fruits won't harm your dragon, but they have a much higher concentration of sugar than fresh fruits, and that is not good.

Nutritional disorders related to inadequate supplementation or mistakes in husbandry, resulting in reduced food intake, may occur in adult dragons, especially those newly acquired by inexperienced owners. Occasionally, oversupplementation occurs when adults are fed large numbers of supplemented crickets daily with products meant to be used only once or twice weekly. Supplements most likely to cause nutrient toxicities are those containing proportionately greater amounts of vitamin A, vitamin D3, and certain trace minerals, including zinc, copper, and iron. Excess calcium intake can lead to constipation and, if prolonged, secondary deficiencies of zinc, copper, and iodine.

Females may consume less food in late pregnancy because the eggs fill much of her coelomic space. During this time, offer the female foods that she especially likes, paying attention to their digestibility and the overall nutritional balance. Crickets and other prey provide more calories and high-quality protein than salads, so supplemented invertebrates may be especially valuable in late stages of pregnancy.

Also pay special attention to the female's diet after egg-laying, as her body's stores need to be replenished quickly. Live invertebrates, especially calcium-dusted superworms for weight gain and hornworms for water content, should be offered two or three times a day in the week following egg-laying. Other prey items the female likes, such as Dubia roaches, silkworms, black soldier fly larvae, and butterworms, can be fed as well. It is also important to continue offering salads, vegetables, and fruit. Right after laying, many females are ravenous, so allow them to eat these foods in whatever quantities they will consume.

SENIOR BEARDED DRAGONS

Recommendations for feeding senior dragons are based on the science of geriatric nutrition. Senior bearded dragons tend to be less active, so they need fewer calories. However, their need for essential nutrients remains nearly the same as those for younger, non-breeding dragons. The goal is to offer fewer calories but to maintain high-quality diets. This is accomplished most easily by offering free-choice, nutritionally balanced salads daily and feeding limited amounts of crickets, superworms, Dubia roaches, black soldier fly larvae, silkworms, hornworms, and butterworms. Adjust feeding frequency and amounts to each dragon's body condition.

FEEDING COMMERCIAL DIETS

A number of commercial diets are marketed specifically for bearded dragons. These are comprised of plant- and animal-based ingredients usually in the form of extruded (and occasionally compressed) pellets. Most contain dyes to enhance colors, and many have sprayed-on odors (marketed erroneously as "flavors") to enhance acceptance by owners as much as by dragons.

Information about testing in feeding trials is limited or lacking. Because the adequacy of these diets is uncertain, a pelleted diet as the sole source of food for bearded dragons is not recommended at this time.

Hand-feeding can enrich the bond between owner and dragon.

DRAGON'S AGE	INSECTS	SALAD	FEEDINGS PER DAY
Babies (0-4 months)	80%	20%	4 or 5, 10 minutes at a time
Juveniles (4-12 months)	70%	30%	3
Sub-adults (12-18 months)	30%	70%	2
Adults (18+ months)	20%	80%	1

Most pellets utilize the ingredients and production techniques of the commercial livestock and pet-food industries. The formulations meet the needs of manufacturing first and dragons second, using ingredients readily available in the feed industry. While these features aren't inherently bad for dragons, they limit the scope and breadth of feeding such enthusiastic, interactive lizards. The ingredients in pellets are relatively few (corn, soy, poultry meal, tallow, alfalfa, wheat, and the like), whereas the palates of bearded dragons range through a myriad of foods. With the exception of alfalfa, a bearded dragon would not normally consume the other ingredients such as corn, soy, etc. The deficiencies in pellet ingredient variety is compensated for by differing shapes and dyes, which may please the eye of the owner more than the palate of bearded dragons. There is also no way to determine the long-term effect of these dyes and other chemicals.

All pellets contain relatively little fat; about 10 or 12 percent is the limit for commercial pellets sold in paper and cardboard containers. Salads contain even less fat. In contrast, invertebrates contain 30–60 percent fat. This fat is essential for bearded dragon nutrition, providing needed calories for growth, reproduction, and good health, along with essential fatty acids for development of vital tissues, especially the brain. Some breeders have observed observe poor growth in juvenile dragons who had been fed low-fat and relatively low-protein pellets. The dragons improved markedly once the diet was changed to a pellet with more fat.

Cranberries
Your bearded dragon may love fresh, cut-up cranberries, and they make a nice fall treat.

Greens will become crispy under the basking light, creating a texture that some beardies enjoy.

In mammalian species, feeding only pellets has led to digestive disorders (in herbivores and omnivores) from a lack of long-stem fibers, poor growth (in omnivores and carnivores) from a lack of fat, and behavioral disorders (in all species) from the monotony of the diet. So owners wishing to feed only pellets to bearded dragons should be cautious and observant.

Although a pellet-only diet is not recommended, if you must feed your dragon a strictly commercial diet with no crickets or salads, wait until it is six months of age, and older is better. The changeover must be gradual, with free-choice offering of the commercial product (offered fresh daily) and gradual removal of other foods over several weeks.

HEALTH PROBLEMS RELATED TO DIET
ASSESSING THE DIET

Owners can assess the adequacy of their dragon's diet by careful observation. A well-fed bearded dragon appears plump and relatively well muscled. There is a slight paunch to the dragon's belly. Pelvic bones should be barely visible in older juveniles and young adults, but the very young, very old, and actively breeding females may exhibit pelvic bones with only a modest covering of subcutaneous fat. Tails should be wide at the base and well fleshed with no bones showing at the tail base. A well-fed dragon is alert and aware of activity in its surroundings. It should actively move about the enclosure to thermoregulate, choosing at various times to bask, eat, dig into substrate, and soak in its water dish. The dragon should eagerly eat live food and enjoy salads too. Stools should be formed rather than sloppy. Like those of other meat-eaters, dragon feces may have a pungent odor, even when the individual is healthy.

An exception to the foregoing description is when the bearded dragon is shutting down for winter brumation but is otherwise healthy. Food intake and activity is greatly reduced in lizards at this time. Weight loss, however, should be minimal.

Developing good observation skills will go a long way in reading your dragon's health. Weighing your beardie every week can alert you to issues early, allowing you time to make corrections before the problem worsens.

WHAT NOT TO FEED

Never place your bearded dragon in a situation where it may be able to catch and ingest something harmful, such as:

- Fireflies (lightning bugs). These are highly toxic to bearded dragons, and ingestion of even one firefly will result in rapid death.
- Spiders known to be venomous to man. If you allow a dragon to spend time outdoors, make sure it will not have access to these venomous spiders, such as black widow and brown recluse spiders.
- Avocado. Because of a chemcial called persin contained in avocado, it is poisonous, even lethal, to pet birds and can have similar effects on bearded dragons. Do not feed any part of an avocado plant to a bearded dragon.
- Wild unidentified mushrooms.
- Unidentified berries.
- Plants known to be toxic to mammals. Avoid houseplants and outdoor plants such as bracken fern, equisetum, buttercup, poppy, rhododendron, foxglove, and the like.
- Foods containing theobromine. These include tea and chocolate.
- Alcohol. On its own or found in some candies, vanilla, and other flavorings.

Handling your dragon and observing its behavior give you important information about its overall health.

- Caffeine. Found in tea, coffee, and some soft drinks.
- Foods with high sugar content or artificial sweeteners. Candy, soft drinks, and sports drinks can lead to digestive and/or metabolic disorders.
- Processed foods. A little nibble of pizza, nachos, or a cheeseburger will likely not harm your bearded dragon, but it's much better to feed your bearded dragon treats from the list of healthy, acceptable foods. In this way, you can strengthen the bond between owner and dragon without risking any potential side effects.

SECONDARY PLANT COMPOUNDS

Plants play a major role in the nutrition of bearded dragons, but they contain much more than just nutrients. A broad category of substances, termed "secondary plant compounds," impacts the feeding of dragons. Some of these substances, oxalates, bind calcium and trace minerals in the digestive tract, preventing their absorption into the bearded dragon's system, thus increasing the risk of nutritional deficiencies.

Oxalates are found in varying amounts in spinach, rhubarb, cabbage, peas, potatoes, beet greens, and many other plants. You do not have to avoid these foods entirely; they are risky only when fed frequently or as the sole source of nutrition without supplementation. Providing the usual supplements of calcium and trace minerals and offering a varied diet eliminates most risk.

Goitrogens are another group of compounds; these bind the trace mineral iodine, risking goiter or hypothyroidism. Goitrogens are found in the highest quantities in cabbage, kale, mustard greens, turnips, rutabagas, and other cruciferous plants, which can be fed as part of a varied diet along with a supplement that contains iodine. The supplement can be as simple as iodized table salt or, even better, iodized "lite" salt, containing iodine, sodium, potassium, and chloride. Many commercial supplements also contain adequate levels of iodine. The mineral iodine is itself toxic in large quantities (also acting as a goitrogen), so take care not to

Did You Know?
Keep in mind that bearded dragons have small stomachs. If you feed your dragon something that is not particularly nutritious, it may be too full to eat the food items that it should be eating. Every bite should count!

overdose with any type of iodine source, whether commercial supplements, iodized salt, or kelp.

There are many other secondary plant compounds, and it is unfortunate that oxalates and goitrogens receive more attention than needed while other substances are ignored. For example, many plants contain substances with hormone-like activity (such as phytoestrogens in soybeans), which may impact bearded dragon reproduction. A large number of different plant fibers may affect digestion and intestinal health. Other compounds in plants influence cognitive function, acting as stimulants or sedatives.

A general rule for feeding plants to bearded dragons is to offer a variety of produce from local markets of the kind and quality that you yourself would eat. Supplement prey items with calcium and other essential nutrients. Also, include an assortment of prey items as part of a varied, balanced diet.

Safe Plant

Pothos, or devil's ivy (if untreated with chemicals), is safe and greatly enjoyed by bearded dragons. However, all plants, including pothos, purchased in stores will have been treated with insecticides at the very least. Soak and rinse the leaves thoroughly before putting pothos in a bearded dragon enclosure.

OTHER FACTORS AFFECTING NUTRITION

The suggestions in this chapter are general guidelines, and many factors will affect the diet and feeding management of bearded dragons in specific situations. For example, those housed outside year-round with exposure to natural sunlight certainly don't need UVB-generating bulbs and may not need a dietary source of vitamin D_3. They may consume trace minerals from the soil

Various factors can affect a dragon's interest in eating.

and an array of secondary plant compounds if offered wild plants. These dragons will have nutritional needs that differ from a pet dragon housed indoors full-time.

You may have to adjust feeding regimens depending on your dragon's condition, its environment, and your management. A change of enclosure or adding cagemates, for example, can alter feeding responses, as can the dragon's attainment of sexual maturity. Adding a cagemate that is not well received can result in one or the other ceasing to eat. If you weigh your dragons each week, you will be alerted to this and can make the proper adjustments. In other words, move one dragon out.

A male, when presented with a female in his enclosure, often ceases all but a minor interest in food because he now has other things on his mind. Even if the male and female are well-paired, she may take over the food consumption, leaving him with very little or nothing. If the male can see another male, he will be distracted by trying to show the potential opponent his ownership by head-bobbing and even ramming into the glass. Food will be of little thought during such situations, so it is wise to observe the dragons during feeding sessions to make sure that all cagemates are eating what they should as well as to block the view of other males from the dragon's enclosure.

Sometimes an owner in a rush will throw a handful of superworms or other prey items into the enclosure and go about their business. In this scenario, the owner risks one dragon eating and the other(s) getting little or nothing. As an owner, you want to know which bearded dragon is eating what.

Females that are bred every year will have greater nutritional demands than a solitary pet that never reproduces. Breeding females are subjected to an obvious stress, and stress itself increases nutrient demands, even in the absence of reproduction. Stress may be insidious and not immediately obvious to bearded dragon owners. For example, stress can arise from chronic excessive exposure to vibrations or light such as TV, video games, phones, too much or rough handling, or unwanted attention by the family dog or cat.

Illness affects nutrition, too. Bearded dragons that are sick or in pain often don't want to eat, which can impair their recovery from illness and surgery. Disease itself impacts nutritional needs, and dragons may lose weight when sick, even though they've maintained their normal food intake. Certain medications can also affect a beardie's appetite, and it might not eat as much while taking medication.

Bearded dragons can be underfed or overfed. Generally, young animals are most at risk for underfeeding because they are growing so rapidly. Juvenile beardies should be allowed to eat as much as they want. Juveniles are growing very fast and will know when they are full. Many cases of underfeeding are due to errors in husbandry, such as incorrect temperatures, dehydration, or insufficient UVB, all of which stimulate the appetites of young dragons.

Older, nonbreeding bearded dragons are most at risk for overfeeding because their growth and activity have slowed. Carefully observe your dragon's body condition accordingly, adjusting the amounts of foods offered to avoid under- and overfeeding. Again, weighing your adult every week will let you know how things are going. An easy way to slim down an older, nonbreeding dragon is to switch from superworms to crickets and Dubia roaches plus salads and vegetables. Offer fruit no more than once a week.

Excessive feeding of snacks and treats risks dietary imbalance and nutritional deficiencies

In multiple-dragon enclosures, make sure each dragon is getting enough to eat.

as well as digestive upsets. Limit snacks to small portions and offer them no more than once or twice weekly. The goal is to limit snacks and treats to about 10 percent of the dragon's total daily food intake.

There is no one right way to feed all bearded dragons. However, observation of your dragon, and consideration of your dragon's living environment and your husbandry methods, will result in a well-fed dragon.

CARE AND STORAGE OF FOOD
POPULAR FEEDER INSECTS

Crickets, Dubia roaches, superworms, and other invertebrates need a balanced diet, too. Balanced diets, when present in the insects' guts, provide nutrients that are absorbed by bearded dragons when the prey is consumed. Don't forget to routinely clean invertebrate enclosures.

Crickets

All bearded dragons love crickets, and babies are mentally stimulated when chasing crickets. Use a 20-gallon (76L) long tank or 66-quart (62L) clear bin to keep 1,000 crickets. When crickets arrive, cut open the box outside (in case you have a few escapees), turn it upside down, and shake the egg crate and crickets into the bin. Once in the bin, the crickets will run from light (the reason for a clear bin as opposed to a solid color) and stay between the egg crate layers. Do not use a lid because it can cause a buildup of condensation, which will kill the crickets and cause a foul odor. Once the crickets are in the bin, feed a commercial cricket food and add a waterer, half of a potato, or greens left over from the dragons' salads for moisture. Old food should be replaced daily. Keep the crickets in a warm room, not in a garage with an extreme temperature. Crickets' calcium-to-phosphorus ratio is stated as 345 to 4313 mg/kg. Dust crickets regularly with calcium powder and periodically with a vitamin/mineral supplement.

A diet including live insects means caring for the insects prior to feeding them to your dragon.

Superworms

Keep 1,000 worms in a plastic sweater box (no lid) with a thick layer of uncooked old-fashioned (not instant) oats. Add gutload in the form of one whole cut potato for moisture and a chunk of acorn squash, carrot, or parsnip to increase calcium and nutritional content. These worms are high in phosphorus, so you must dust them thoroughly with a calcium supplement and by gutloading with high-calcium foods. Also, feed superworms to your dragons less frequently than other insects. Bearded dragon subadults and adults love superworms, especially freshly shed white worms. The calcium-to-phosphorus ratio is 124 to 2356 mg/kg.

Dubia Roaches

Some babies and adults relish these feeder insects. Stated values from one breeder are 312 mg/kg calcium and 840 mg/kg phosphorus. One reason Dubia roaches became very popular feeder insects is that feeding colonies are easy to establish. Start a colony with a ratio of one male to four females, in a dark-colored plastic storage tote with a lid. Cut a rectangle out of one side and hot-glue a piece of window screen over the hole to provide air. There are differing opinions on what to feed the roaches, but a colony will do well and breed well on high-quality, high-protein fish flakes, cucumber, high-calcium greens, and leftover veggies. You can also feed them roach chow and give them cucumbers for water.

Place a heating pad set at medium under one side of the tote; alternatively, you can use heat tape. There is no substrate. Clean the frass (roach feces) out every few months. Either use a respirator or clean the bin in a well-ventilated area. The dust that becomes airborne while cleaning could be unpleasant at the very least.

Many beardies like mealworms, but they are not recommended.

Dust the roaches with calcium before feeding them to the dragons. A Dubia roach colony is also a great backup for emergencies when crickets are not available due to a weather-related emergency or for some other unexpected circumstance.

Black Soldier Fly Larvae

These are the easiest feeder insects because they require no maintenance (no feeding, water, or cleaning). It is not necessary to keep them refrigerated. Place on a shelf in a room, and they will be fine for two to three weeks. Some will become black, but they are not dead and still can be fed.

Phoenix Worms (a brand of black soldier fly larvae) can be plumped in water and fed to a dehydrated dragon for a quick fix, and they are arguably the highest feeder insect in calcium along with butterworms. The calcium-to-phosphorus ratio is 1.5 to 1—very high in calcium—with 17.3 percent protein. It is claimed that there is no need to dust them with calcium. There are many sources of black soldier fly larvae, but Phoenix Worms have the proper calcium-to-phosphorus ratio and the ability to "plump."

Silkworms

Silkworms are soft-bodied feeder insects that can be purchased online from suppliers. They have very high moisture and protein content, at 76 percent and 64 percent, respectively. They eat only silkworm chow, which is made from mulberry leaves. Most bearded dragons just love silkworms. Their high moisture content helps the dragons stay hydrated.

Hornworms

Hornworms are also relished by bearded dragons. Hornworms are also grown on special hornworm chow. They have a high moisture content of 85 percent, with 9 percent protein. Hornworms come in both green and blue, and most beardies prefer green.

Butterworms

Butterworms are very high in calcium, and some bearded dragons love them. They are packed in bran in a cup, and you keep them in the refrigerator. They have a decent "shelf life" of one to two months.

Waxworms

Waxworms are OK for larger dragons on occasion. They are very high in fat, and some bearded dragons go crazy for them and refuse to eat other feeder insects. Keep small quantities of waxworms in the refrigerator. If you intend to raise waxworms, you need to feed them a special diet that includes glycerin, honey, ground cereals, and brewer's yeast. The calcium-to-phosphorus ratio is stated to be 46 to 489 mg/kg.

Did You Know?

Hornworms can sometimes be found on your tomato plants, but please do not feed those worms to bearded dragons. Hornworms found on tobacco plants or tomato plants are highly toxic to bearded dragons.

Mealworms

Usually, large quantities of mealworms are maintained on bran, and you can purchase a small cup of them that you keep in the refrigerator. Some pet owners feed mealworms, but there are some reasons not to. First, babies and juveniles cannot digest them, and even adults may have trouble digesting them properly. Further, they take a long time to digest, so you cannot feed mealworms to your beardies too late in the day. Mealworms are also very high in chitin (shell), fat, and phosphorus in relation to

Mealworm larvae

beneficial nutrients. There are so many healthy feeder insects to choose from that feeding mealworms is unnecessary. The only upside is that mealworms are cheap. The calcium-to-phosphorus ratio is stated to be 68 to 491 mg/kg.

PRODUCE

Wash fresh fruits and vegetables prior to feeding, especially if you suspect that they were sprayed with herbicides or pesticides. Buy organic when you can. Check produce from the grocery store carefully for hazardous materials, such as twist ties, bits of plastic, and rubber bands; these items can lead to life-threatening digestive problems. Remove sticky labels from the surfaces of apples, pears, and the like. Frozen vegetables marketed for human consumption are a good option, too, because they are well preserved with little loss of vitamins and other nutrients. Thaw frozen vegetables before feeding.

SUPPLEMENTS

Keep in mind that supplements have limited shelf lives. Many vitamins decompose from exposure to light, air, and heat—so don't keep supplement containers on top of your dragons' enclosure because the heat drifts upward and will degrade your supplements faster. Some types of supplements are oxidized by contact with trace minerals. Select products with expiration dates and replace supplements at least every four months.

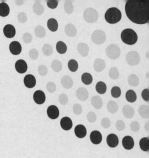

What Are High-Quality Greens and Produce?

Freshly picked greens and vegetables have the highest levels of nutrition, and locally grown produce is a good choice. If you are so inclined, you can cut down on your food costs and increase the nutritional value of greens by growing your own. Some greens, like arugula and endive, are harvestable in as little as thirty days, and you can even grow greens in pots if you have no space. For apartment dwellers, a few pots on a patio or balcony will afford you fresh greens for your dragon all summer. There are no greens your bearded dragon will love more than those that are freshly picked, and they offer the highest nutritional value. Store-bought greens and produce shipped in from other countries just do not have the same nutritional content.

You can also grow strawberries, bell peppers, and bush-type green beans in pots. If you have more space, you can easily construct a simple 4- x 8-foot (1.2 x 2.4m) raised bed out of lumber and deck screws or from a kit. In either case, fill the bed with good soil. It is as easy as that. Next thing you know, you will have the convenience of dragon food at your door. Having greens right there will keep your dragon supplied with fresh foods even if you cannot get to a store.

CHAPTER 6

THE BEARDED DRAGON AS A PET

So just how good are bearded dragons as pets? The answer? They might just be the best reptile pets!

Unlike many other lizards, dragons almost never bite their handlers, scratch when held, or whip with their tails when approached. They offer unique and charming personalities and natural curiosity about the world around them, including their owners. As your dragon matures, you'll find it making eye contact with you, approaching you for treats, and remaining quiet and friendly when held for short periods. Some will form serious bonds

Children can take part in the bearded dragon's care.

with their owners like any beloved pet. Sometimes the bond becomes so strong that the dragon will not eat when the owner is absent. Other dragons will demonstrate with their actions that they want to be taken out of the enclosure and held by the person they've bonded with.

Bearded dragons are ideal because they provide the pleasure and entertainment of a pet that enjoys, but doesn't always require, interaction with humans. Unlike other pets, such as dogs and parrots, they won't develop neuroses if they're not handled or given attention daily. Bearded dragons are sizeable but not too large. They're aesthetically complex and different enough to draw attention. They are available in an array of gorgeous colors. They are also characters that can demonstrate endearing signs of intelligence and responsiveness.

In terms of care, drawbacks may include their need for a relatively large enclosure, proper lighting and temperature, and insects for food. For those who do not care for live insects, there are now options that make this a nonissue. As mentioned, black soldier fly larvae do not need to be refrigerated, fed, or gutloaded and are very nutritious for your dragon.

Bearded dragons require maintenance of about ten or fifteen minutes a day. So if that amount of time is something you can handle, there will be no experience like owning a bearded dragon. They are completely addictive. With such an array of colors to choose from and the fact that each beardie has a unique and special personality, it is easy to see why many owners wind up with more than one.

HANDLING

Hatchlings and baby bearded dragons are fragile and can be crushed easily, so they should not be handled (except for health checks) until they are at least 8 inches (20cm) long. Be careful with all juveniles because they can be seriously hurt if they fall onto hard surfaces or even fall from something in their tank or enclosure. This is another good reason to keep the juvenile setup simple. During the first eight weeks of a dragon's life, the most responsiveness you should expect is food taken from your hand or tweezers. If a baby dragon happens to climb on you, great, but keep your hand within the enclosure in case he jumps off.

After a bearded dragon reaches a length of 8 inches (20cm), you will be able to handle it more frequently, but only for a brief period each time. In terms of handling, bearded dragons don't enjoy long-term holding and petting; plus, their skin is rough to the touch and not that inviting to pet anyway. If physical contact with a pet is important to you, you might consider a leatherback bearded dragon, whose skin is smoother than that of normal-scaled dragons. If you prefer the dinosaur-like appearance of spikes, then a normal-scaled bearded dragon is a good option.

In either case, you do not need to "tame" a bearded dragon. Most juveniles are naturally skittish, with a healthy fight-or-flight mechanism. Bearded dragons are skittish as youngsters because everything in Australia—including larger bearded dragons—eats baby bearded dragons! A healthy fear response

is a good sign. As the babies grow (and they grow quickly), they will be higher on the food chain and become less fearful and more relaxed. Plus, once the dragons get to know you as the "food person," they will gradually come to trust you.

If you are a gentle keeper to your dragon, it will naturally want that bond to continue. On the other hand, if you continually grab at the dragon, attempting to "tame" it, the dragon may never lose its fear of you, thus damaging any bond or chance that it will grow to trust you. Improper handling is what causes some bearded dragons to grow up to resent their owners. As with any animal, how you treat your bearded dragon early on determines much about its behavior as an adult.

Take care when handling your dragon that he does not jump down from a height.

Never allow your bearded dragon to be loose outdoors, even if perched on a shoulder. It can fall or become frightened and dart off. If it escapes, it will be easy prey for dogs, cats, large birds, and raccoons, and it runs a big risk of being run over by a car. If you must carry your adult bearded dragon around with you, invest in a lizard harness and leash.

If you plan to take your dragon outside or anywhere in public, remember that many people are afraid of reptiles. Be respectful of people's wishes regarding how close they want to be to your beardie. Your responsible actions as a bearded dragon owner can help people have positive experiences with reptiles.

HAND-FEEDING

Bearded dragons are not drawn to humans because of social propensity (in the way that dogs look to their owners as their leaders) or because they enjoy physical contact or good conversation—but this is not to say that many bearded dragons don't have special relationships with their owners, because many of them can and do. Remember that as juveniles, your dragons will first connect with you as the "food person." Bearded dragons quickly learn to associate their owners with food.

Regularly offering your bearded dragon food held by your fingertips or in the palm of your hand (hand-feeding) is important for establishing a positive relationship between owner and dragon. Hand-feeding can be done when bearded dragons are just a few weeks old. In time, they will learn to come toward you as you approach the enclosure because they begin to associate you with tasty goodies.

You can hand-feed a large subadult or an adult to ensure that the dragon is getting the right mix of foods in its diet. Sometimes a beardie will develop a liking for one particular food and won't eat the other foods offered. Hand-feeding is a way to make sure that your dragon gets the mix of foods it needs. A little treat at the end can serve as encouragement to eat what you offer. Just like children, bearded dragons can learn that they do not get the treat until they finish the vegetables.

DRAGON HYGIENE AND GROOMING

No matter how large you make your dragon's living quarters, an enclosure still isn't the wide open space of the great outdoors. A pet dragon remains in relatively close proximity to its excreted feces and urine, leftover food, fouled water, and old substrate. Such close contact can make for a soiled dragon and can even pose a risk for disease at times. This is why cleanliness is so important.

In addition to keeping the cage clean, you'll want to keep your dragon clean. You can bathe a dragon that is soiled with feces or bedding. Place your dragon in a plastic container (such as a plastic storage tub) containing an inch or two (2 to 5cm) of warm water; soap is unnecessary. Using a soft toothbrush, nail brush, or washcloth, gently wash the dirty areas. Wash in the direction of the scales, not against them. Once you are finished, rinse the dragon in clean, warm water. **Note:** Once a brush or cloth is designated for dragon use, never use it again on humans.

Different dragons may prefer different temperatures for their bath water. If your dragon jumps out of the water like a cat, try warmer (not hot) water. You will know when you've found your dragon's preferred temperature, because it will relax and brighten in color.

Soak large subadult and adult bearded dragons three times a week and mist them in their enclosures daily to keep them well hydrated and their skin healthy. Some adult bearded dragons like water deep enough to do laps in. In those cases, offer the swimmers a deeper pool that still allows the dragons to touch their toes on the bottom. Supervise your beardie at all times. Bearded dragons can drown!

Do not bathe babies unless they soil themselves, but do mist them twice a day: thirty minutes after the lights go on in the morning and thirty minutes before the lights go out at night. In the morning, mist with hot water, and use warm water at night. If a baby runs away from the mist, the water is likely too cold.

A bearded dragon will shed its skin in small patches routinely throughout the year, and this is a normal process. Young bearded dragons will shed many more times than an adult. A young dragon up to six months old may shed weekly. Between six and twelve months, this will slow to every couple weeks, then to every couple months. As an adult, your beardie will shed a couple times a year.

Shedding is a natural process that happens throughout the year.

Don't be surprised by the way your dragon sheds. Beardies don't shed all at once, like snakes do. Instead, the body, head, and limbs all shed at their own rate. You don't need to assist the dragon by peeling off loose skin, and you should refrain from the temptation to use hand lotions and oils on a dragon's skin. The loose skin will shed in its own time, at the right time. Peeling skin that is not ready to come off can damage the new skin underneath.

Occasionally, shed skin may become stuck around the tail and toes, in which case your dragon will need assistance because the bands of dead skin can constrict the blood flow, leading to the death of cells in the extremities, which can cause the loss of a toe or tail tip. Soaking and gently peeling often removes stubborn rings of skin. If the skin doesn't come off, take your dragon to a qualified veterinarian. If this problem recurs frequently, review your overall husbandry, especially humidity levels and access to water.

There are products on the market formulated to help reptiles shed. These products do work as skin conditioners but are not necessary because properly misting and soaking adult dragons will adequately hydrate their skin.

Another aspect of bearded dragon grooming is nail care. Dragons' nails stay short and strong if exposed to rocks and coarse pebbles. Dragons that live on soft surfaces may need their long nails clipped regularly. The staff at your veterinarian's office can perform this task for you, or you can clip the nails yourself, using a small nail clipper made for cats. Always have coagulant powder, such as Kwik Stop, handy. Remove just the tip of the nail, taking care to avoid the quick (vein), which is much easier to see on hypomelanistic (clear-nailed) bearded dragons. For dragons with dark nails, err on the side of caution and remove just the sharp tip. If the nail bleeds, apply coagulant powder or styptic pencil and try taking less off each remaining nail.

BRUMATION IN PET DRAGONS

At about one or two years of age, bearded dragons will go through a winter "hibernation" period known as brumation. Some bearded dragons are sleepy and reduce their food intake, while others will go through a major

Shedding Aid
Facilitate shedding by placing a 6-by-6-inch (15-by-15cm) square section of cardboard egg carton in the enclosure and misting the adult dragon on top of the cardboard. The water soaks the egg carton, and the dragons love to rub themselves against the rough, wet cardboard, which helps shed dead skin.

shutdown and cannot be wakened. Usually, brumation begins in late fall/early winter, when there is less daylight. The following paragraphs detail how to handle the brumation period for dragons kept indoors and in enclosures. Keep in mind that breeders seem to have their own ways of handling brumation, and much depends on the local climate, how many dragons are kept, and if they are indoors or outside. Each living situation and each dragon is different, but the following information should serve as a helpful general guide.

PREPARING

In preparation for brumation, weigh your dragon each week, starting in August, if you have not already made weekly weigh-ins a habit. It is a good idea to visit the veterinarian in September/early fall for a checkup and a fecal flotation to check for coccidia and intestinal parasites. Bearded dragons are at a weakened state during brumation, and any illnesses can cause serious trouble. If parasites take over while your dragon sleeps, the dragon may not recover. Intestinal parasites, such as pinworms, are fairly easy to cure with Panacur and scrupulous daily cage and water-bowl cleaning with a bleach-and-water solution. Coccidia is often treated with Ponazuril and requires the same attention to cage and water-bowl cleanliness.

A bearded dragon's nails need attention to stay short and strong.

CARE DURING BRUMATION

Remember, each beardie approaches brumation differently. Some shut down entirely, not eating or drinking for six weeks or longer. Other dragons are sleepy but still wake up once or twice a week to drink or eat a little. For these dragons, turn basking temperatures down to 80°F (27°C) and the cool side to about 65°F (18°C), keep the lights on for only eight hours during the day, and turn all lights off at night. If a dragon is not eating at all, is sound asleep, hasn't eaten or drunk for ten days or so, and is not defecating but is maintaining weight, shut all of the lights off for the entire brumation period. To ensure that they are maintaining weight, carefully weigh the dragons every two weeks but try to disturb them as little as possible.

You can give your dragon a cardboard shoe box that has one short side cut out and that has been misted on the inside. A dragon that wants to go into a deep sleep will love this.

WAKE-UP TIME

After eight weeks, resume keeping the lights on for twelve hours a day, increase the basking spot temperature to 100°F (38°F), and increase the cool side floor to 80°F (27°F). Weigh your dragon and soak it twice a day in warm water for fifteen minutes at a time. Begin feeding lightly with high-water greens, such as romaine lettuce, until the dragon begins to defecate normally. After about three days, it should be fine to resume feeding invertebrates, such as crickets, superworms, and other prey items, as well as vegetables and fruits.

TROUBLE WAKING

Sometimes sleepy bearded dragons have trouble waking up and are very slow to regain their appetites. In this case, start feeding your dragon lightly, as previously mentioned, feeling for any kind of impaction or hard lump until the animal defecates. It can take some dragons weeks to get back into the normal rhythm. The most important thing is to keep the dragon hydrated. If your dragon is not drinking during its soaks or during misting, keep up with the fifteen-minute soaks once or twice a day, in the early morning and/or late evening.

You can implement supportive care in the form of reptile electrolytes or Pedialyte (any flavor) mixed with a spoonful of strained baby food, either chicken or beef, until it is the

Back to Normal

A bearded dragon in a true, deep brumation will usually form a fecal plug because he is not eating or drinking. Once the dragon starts eating again, it will expel the plug in its feces.

consistency of pudding. Use an oral syringe or eye dropper to administer the mixture: while holding the dragon, smear some of the mixture on his lips, being careful not to cover the nostrils. The dragon will lick it off. Keep offering the mixture in this way until it is finished. Do this two or three times a day initially, and add a pinch of vitamin and calcium supplements once a day. This type of supportive care helps get the bowels going.

Another method of getting dragons to eat is to offer hornworms or silkworms purchased from a supplier. These insects are high in water and can successfully jump-start a dragon who is slow to come around after brumation.

TRAVELING WITH YOUR BEARDED DRAGON

During your bearded dragon's lifetime, it is likely that your pet will have to travel. You may need to visit the veterinarian's office, your beardie may accompany you to school for a project, or your family might move to a new home.

Bearded dragons travel well inside small plastic cat carriers, which are available wherever pet supplies are sold. It's best to purchase the carrier ahead of time so that you can acclimate your dragon to the new smells and confined space. Place an old bath towel, paper towels, or newspaper in the bottom of the carrier. If you use a towel, make sure that your dragon's nails have been trimmed; otherwise, a sharp nail can catch on a loop of thread, and your dragon may rip his entire nail off in the course of trying to disentangle it. You want your dragon's time inside the carrier to be positive!

Start with short sessions of just a minute or two. Place your dragon inside the carrier with one of its favorite snacks. Leave the door open and stay right there with your pet. If your dragon panics, don't force the issue. Let him come out of the carrier and give him time to calm down. Try again in an hour or so. As your dragon relaxes in the carrier, training sessions can last longer and you can practice with the door shut. As your dragon learns to associate the carrier with tasty food, he'll look forward to climbing in and staying put.

Be sure to label your carrier with pertinent information. Create a label that includes your name, address, and phone number. You might also want to include, in large letters, the words "HARMLESS REPTILE."

If you have other pets in the household, don't let your bearded dragon get into a potentially dangerous situation.

Here are a few points to remember when traveling with dragons:

- Dragons quickly overheat and die if left in a closed car on a warm or sunny day.
- Call ahead if you plan to travel by air. Many airlines won't allow reptiles in the cabin at any time or reptiles in cargo during hot weather. Don't try to sneak onto the plane with your dragon. If your dragon does travel in cargo, special packing and insulation are essential.
- Bring food and especially water from home. Strange smells can inhibit a dragon from consuming different foods and water. You may wish to also bring along your dragon's usual dishes for food and water.
- Plan on changing the carrier's bedding daily. Bring extra toweling.
- Remember that some people are afraid of reptiles. Don't frighten people with your dragon.
- Don't inadvertently frighten hotel housekeeping staff with your dragon. When traveling with your dragons, request that your room not be serviced and leave a "Do Not Disturb" sign on the door. Simply pick up fresh towels as needed from housekeeping.
- Hotel rooms, rugs, and bathtubs may have been treated with chemicals and insecticides.
- Lawns and foliage growing at rest stops, golf courses, city parks, and suburban yards are likely to have been treated with chemicals.

Don't forget: Your dragon will overheat and die if left in a closed car on a warm or sunny day. Be extra careful when traveling with your dragon.

Sometimes, taking your dragon with you is just not feasible. You'll either need a pet sitter or you'll have to board your pet. If you want to board your

Did You Know?

You can also use the baby food/electrolyte mixture for a newly acquired dragon that may not be eating after the trip home due to "travel shock." If the enclosure is correct in terms of basking and cool-side floor temperatures, it's worth a try. Offer the mixture twice a day, and you should see results. You should not have to do this for more than two days.

Though your dragon may enjoy exploring, it's best not to let it loose outside.

pet, start your search in advance to find facilities in your area that will take a bearded dragon. It is likely that you will need to provide all supplies, from habitat to food, but make sure the staff at the boarding facility understands the care of a beardie. Is someone going to add supplements? Do they understand the importance of lighting and heat? Are they OK with handling live food? Will they interact with your dragon? If not, you may need a pet sitter.

Family and friends are probably the best place place to start, as they may already be familiar with the needs of your beardie, but you should still leave written notes, including the name and number of your veterinarian. No matter if your sitter is family or a professional pet sitter, write down everything so they don't overlook any part of the routine. Note when to turn lights on and off. Ask that they spot-clean the enclosure daily. If you're going to be gone for an extended period, detail how you deep-clean. Remind your sitter to check temperatures daily. If they don't know how to bathe your dragon, have a hands-on session.

Leave spare bulbs for your lights. Prepare individual salads in storage bags so that your sitter has easy access to the correct blend and portions. If the sitter is uncomfortable with roaches or crickets, use black soldier fly larvae. Depending on how long you will be away, you can even pre-measure the larvae into individual paper cups. All of this preparation not only helps your sitter but also can give you peace of mind, knowing that you've done all you can to assure that your dragon is cared for properly while you're away.

EMERGENCY PLANNING FOR DRAGONS

As much as you may try to avoid it, disaster can strike. Depending on the part of the country you live in, you may be vulnerable to earthquakes, blizzards, hurricanes, ice storms, tornadoes, floods, or fire. When there's a bearded dragon in the family, disaster preparedness includes planning for your dragon's welfare.

To begin, plan how your dragon would survive for at least a week if you could not leave your home. Fortunately, dragons are omnivorous and can survive on salads and snacks when live prey is not available. Owners have fed their dragons everything from granola to dry dog and cat food to thawed veggies and meats during times of crisis. A better idea is to have several cans of Can O' Crickets or Can O' Grasshoppers (depending on your dragon's age and size) in store as well as black soldier fly larvae, which does not need to be refrigerated. Vacuum-sealed insects are another way to keep some food handy. These go-to items are healthier for your dragon than dog food. Avoid freeze-dried products. The insects are starved prior to freezing so that any food in them will not rot. They offer no moisture and no real protein.

Dragons can survive several days of fasting, but they need water every day. Stock a few extra gallons of bottled water so your dragon has a supply of fresh water for drinking and soaking. As with all living creatures, water is more important than food.

Maybe you're not house-bound, but the power has gone out. Move your dragon to a smaller container where it will be easier to keep him warm. Put a towel in the bottom of the container, then cover the container with a blanket or heavy towel to keep warmth in. Check the temperature regularly. You may need to tape heat packs to the side of the container. Hand warmers will work, as will medical heat packs. You may feed salads but don't feed insects until your dragon can once again bask.

Next, consider what to do if you are ordered to evacuate. Generally, there are two types of plans you should think about: how to evacuate with your dragon, and how to leave your dragon behind if necessary for your own survival and that of human family members. When there's an emergency, never risk your safety, even if it means leaving your dragon behind.

When an emergency hits, you won't have the time or presence of mind to formulate a plan for your bearded dragon. Plan now, and consider all of the following points:

- Keep a plastic cat carrier handy for transporting and temporarily housing your dragon.
- Make a list of simple instructions for feeding and watering your dragon, along with its needs for light and heat and your cell number. Post a copy of these

Your dragon is a valued part of your family, so include it in any emergency plans.

instructions by a door to the house and by the dragon's enclosure. Keep these notes simple so that neighbors or disaster personnel can follow them if you can't get home because of an emergency.

- If you evacuate and cannot bring your dragon, post a note in indelible ink by the door most frequently used and in a location that will be seen by emergency personnel entering your house. Provide your name, where you can be found, and contact numbers for friends or family who are likely to know your whereabouts. If your dragon is in the house, state its location and emphasize that it is a harmless lizard.

- Keep with you the phone numbers of your veterinarian, reptile-keeping friends, and the local herpetological society or zoo. Remember, though, that everyone else is also dealing with the disaster and may be unable to help you. Also take along phone numbers for your insurance agent, your attorney, and the police, fire department, and Red Cross.

- If your dragon is likely to be chilled because of power outages or living in a motel or shelter, don't feed it. Wait until you can warm the lizard.

- Your dragon may need a veterinary checkup when the emergency ends, especially if it has been exposed to cold temperatures, smoke, fouled water, dehydration, or long periods of fasting. Dragons are hardy souls, but they'll appreciate the attention after surviving a disaster.

- If your house catches on fire, get out! Don't stop for your dragon. Don't think you'll have the time or luck. Get out immediately.

SAYING GOOD-BYE

Someday, you and your dragon may part ways. You may lose interest in the lizard or be dealing with circumstances that demand placement of your pet in another home. Here is some advice if you can no longer care for your dragon:

- Never turn your dragon loose. It will not survive for long, and the time spent until its death will be filled with terror and pain. Your dragon is no longer a wild animal and cannot fend for itself, whether in the city, suburbs, country, park, or wilderness area.

- Call the closest zoos and herpetological societies. They often know of those who place reptiles in good homes.
- You may wish to advertise your dragon for sale in a local newspaper or on a community bulletin board or online forum. Be sure to interview prospective buyers and select the one you think will give your dragon the best home and care. Be careful, though, of those with not-so-honest intentions. In one case, an owner posted his dragon on Craigslist and received an immediate reply. The would-be buyer turned out to be a collector of large snakes who was looking for free or cheap food for his snakes!

Sometimes, you must make even more difficult decisions. Your dragon may become seriously ill or very old. Helping a beloved pet die humanely with minimal pain, stress, or fear is part of responsible ownership and the last gift that you can give your dragon. Here are some pointers:

- Never try to induce death in your dragon by putting it in the freezer or by withholding food and water. These practices are inhumane and will cause your dragon much pain and suffering.
- Consult with your veterinarian. Humane euthanasia is inexpensive and causes minimal suffering. Your veterinarian may offer advice as to the value of a necropsy (animal autopsy) and services such as cremation. If you wish, you can return home with your dragon's body for burial, receive its ashes for later burial, or let the vet dispose of the body. Don't throw the body out in the trash.

Owners of bearded dragons that die go through a grieving process similar to that which occurs when a human friend or family member is lost. Some friends or associates may not understand your loss. "After all, it was only a lizard." Do not believe them. Grieving over the loss of a beloved bearded dragon is very real. There are pet grief counselors and hotlines that can help. In time, you'll remember just the joy of owning a dragon, and you may consider once again opening your heart and home to another bearded dragon.

CHAPTER 7

BEARDED DRAGON BEHAVIORS

Compared to many lizards, inland bearded dragons display a wide range of social behaviors. For obvious reasons, they will only display the full range of these behaviors once they reach sexual maturity and if they are kept in a group. This chapter discusses some of the behaviors you will notice in this species.

SOCIAL HIERARCHIES

In the wild or in captivity, bearded dragons raised in a group form social hierarchies relatively early in life. Using the terminology of animal behavior, the leader of any group is called the "alpha" animal.

If you raise a group of baby bearded dragons, it quickly becomes apparent that some individuals are "top dogs," while others are submissive. During the immature stages, you'll usually see a clear distinction between several of the more dominant individuals (rather than one alpha animal) and the more submissive dragons. The dominant dragons are more vigorous in their feeding behaviors and intimidate smaller, more submissive animals.

Adult bearded dragons can coexist peacefully within their established hierarchy.

As a pattern, bearded dragons that are aggressive feeders grow faster, which makes them need to eat more, which makes them even more aggressive feeders, grabbing increasing portions of the food offered. They are the alphas of the group. These dominant dragons are often at the top of the basking area, sitting on the prime spot. You will often observe these dragons looking sideways at the more submissive dragons, almost giving them the "evil eye," daring them to come and eat.

Over time, the intimidated smaller animals wisely become wary of the quick and daring feeding behaviors of

A darkened body increases heat absorption.

the larger ones and thus have less access to food. They end up eating less and remaining smaller unless moved to separate rearing containers.

Dominant juvenile bearded dragons, if hungry and underfed, often turn to mutilating the tail tips, digits, and even lower limbs of less dominant animals. Larger immature bearded dragons may also attempt to eat smaller ones. In the world of bearded dragons, the first months of life are a ruthless race to feed and grow to a large size.

Once bearded dragons mature, their new reproduction-related behaviors kick in. Social hierarchies become more defined, and a large male becomes the alpha animal of the group.

THERMOREGULATION

There's another reason you should keep dragons separate: their need to bask. Frequently, as a show of dominance, one dragon will lie on top of the other. This effectively blocks the lower dragon from any heat.

Another interesting fact related to thermoregulation is the importance of the beardie's third, or parietal, eye. Besides being connected to the pineal gland and helping to regulate hormones, this "eye," which does have a vestigial retina and lens, helps the dragon find heat. It also offers an early warning system if a predator (or your hand) is overhead—which is why you should always reach for your dragon from underneath.

Like most reptiles, bearded dragons can raise their body temperatures relatively quickly, but they cool down slowly and cannot readily cool themselves to below air temperature. The preferred daytime body temperature of bearded dragons is around 98°F (37°C), which they can easily achieve by basking in sunlight, even at air temperatures 10°F (6°C) or more cooler than the target body temperature.

Climbing and Basking-Site Hierarchies

In the wild, inland bearded dragons are considered semi-arboreal animals and will readily climb shrubs, rock piles, and fallen tree trunks when available. These raised structures often form the topographical nucleus of a group of bearded dragons.

In the wild and in well-designed greenhouse enclosures, bearded dragons compete for prime basking areas, which are usually the highest and most easily accessible sites, such as fence posts, fallen trees, shrubs, or rock outcrops. Typically, the alpha male of a group acquires the top position on a basking site. Outdoors, the higher a dragon climbs, the higher it is on the social ladder.

Bearded dragons flatten and darken their bodies to increase heat absorption and quickly raise their body temperatures when exposed to sunlight. Bearded dragons can also warm their bodies by absorbing radiant heat from warm surfaces, such as rocks or the ground. In the wild, as midday air temperatures rise toward 103°F (40°C), bearded dragons usually remain hidden and sheltered from the sun because of their limited ability to cool down below air temperature.

For this reason, it is very important that the basking site in an enclosure is offset by a cooler section, as previously mentioned. Bearded dragons that are heated day and night with one or more spotlights and heat strips running the length of a vivarium can become heat-stressed and die suddenly. The importance of a cooler sheltered area in the upper upper 70s to low 80s Fahrenheit (mid- to upper 20s Celsius) during the day cannot be emphasized enough. Bearded dragons need a gradient of 20°F (11°C) from the basking spot to cool side floor.

GAPING OR PANTING WHEN BASKING

Some bearded dragons choose to remain at high temperatures and may gape (keep the mouth open) or pant (keep the mouth open while performing throat movements to increase the rate of air flow in and out of the mouth and lungs) while basking. Dragons also gape in the initial stages of overheating, presumably in an attempt to cool down. Gaping should not concern owners unless the dragons' enclosure is overheated and fails to provide cool areas. If the enclosure is too hot, the owner should turn off the heat sources and adjust the enclosure's design to provide a heat gradient of 20°F (11°C). Gaping and forced exhalation may also occur in bearded dragons with respiratory infections, with lung damage from inhaling too much dust, or with certain types of parasite infection. Clearly, the owner must interpret the cause of gaping in the context of husbandry, often with a veterinarian's help.

OPEN-MOUTH BEARDED DISPLAYS

A bearded dragon hatchling performs the classic display of an open mouth with beard extended toward large moving objects that it interprets as threats. It is easy to see how this defensive display earned these lizards their common name.

In captivity, most bearded dragons readily habituate to movements by their caretakers, so the propensity to perform the open-mouth display quickly wanes. Nonetheless, the potential to perform this display remains throughout the life of a bearded dragon.

Eastern bearded dragons tend to perform this display much more readily than inland bearded dragons and are not as likely to habituate to large moving objects. However, any suddenly startled individual may perform a bearded display, and individuals who are considered aggressive do so even more readily.

Higher temperatures will usually increase the likelihood of a bearded dragon performing a bearded display. Additionally, no matter how habituated a bearded dragon may become to humans, suddenly exposing the dragon to certain

A bearded display from a wild bearded dragon in the Australian desert.

Tail Curling

Bearded dragons commonly adopt a position in which most of the tail is curled up above the ground as they remain still. This is a sign of being on alert and is commonly performed by adult bearded dragons throughout the day.

animals, such as snakes and monitors, seems to readily elicit the display. Since many of these animals prey on bearded dragons in the wild, this open-mouth behavior is likely a fear response.

MUTILATION/CANNIBALISM

Juvenile bearded dragons may mutilate their cagemates. This behavior is most readily performed by Stage 2 (hatchling) animals—larger or dominant individuals—toward more passive bearded dragons when not enough food is available. Hungry, more assertive individuals may bite off tail tips, toes, and sections of limbs of smaller dragons. In extreme cases, when a smaller dragon is of gobbling size, more dominant juveniles may attempt and succeed at cannibalism.

Even in larger dragons, specific conditions can result in a significant level of mutilation. Limited food availability and overcrowded conditions can be contributing factors.

If you plan to breed bearded dragons, keep babies in individual baby bins. The alternative is to constantly monitor the dragons' behaviors and move babies that are lower in the social hierarchy to other baby bins with more submissive animals; this must be done daily or even more often as aggressive behavior is observed.

Large adults seldom mutilate other dragons of similar size. Close observation of bearded dragons usually reveals that when mutilation does occur in a group of subadults, often one individual is responsible for the damage. Within a group, if the conditions leading to mutilation persist, the end result is usually one able and actively feeding individual and several injured and crippled dragons. If you plan on having multiple dragons, keep them all safe by giving each its own individual enclosure.

ARM-WAVING

Arm-waving is the earliest social behavior in bearded dragons, and it can be witnessed within days of hatching. It serves both as an intraspecies signal (basically, "I'm a bearded dragon") and as an appeasement gesture ("please don't hurt me"). It persists as an appeasement/submissive gesture in adult females during breeding with her preferred male. More rarely it is performed by submissive males when more aggressive males bite their necks. Juvenile bearded dragons will often wave at their new owners. It is an endearing trait that has won over many a pet owner.

HEAD-BOBBING OR HEAD-JERKING

Head-bobbing refers to a lowering and quick raising of the dragon's head, usually performed in repetitive sets. The lifting component of the behavior can be so vigorous that the entire front of the dragon's body jerks upward. This behavior (called head-jerking by some) is most often seen when males are in breeding/territorial mode, usually exhibiting a black beard. This is a sexual display performed as a part of courtship toward females prior to copulation.

Weighing your pet dragon or dragons weekly can alert you to problems early on, before they become too serious. A sudden drop of 15–20 grams in a week for no apparent reason is a prime example. Examine the enclosure's temperatures, setup, and anything new that may have caused this change, and see a veterinarian. Ask the vet to include a fecal flotation to test for coccidia and intestinal worms; this simple test could save your dragon's life. Bearded dragons are excellent at hiding illnesses, which likely is a defense mechanism to keep from alerting predators that the dragon is in a weakened state. Early action on your part may prevent a tragedy. By weighing your dragons weekly, you may prevent this from happening to you. Weigh-in time also gives you the opportunity to give the dragon a once-over and check its eyes, trim its nails, and check its skin.

Females in breeding mode will respond to this behavior by slowly lowering and raising her head below him. If a female is placed with a male, but she is not ready for breeding, she will often raise her head as high as possible to signal that she is not accepting him. She may also perform this behavior if she is placed with a male she does not prefer.

In captivity, dominance behavior can lead to stress and other problems.

MALE-MALE ENCOUNTERS

In the wild, male-to-male encounters and occasional male-male fights occur. These fights are mostly ritualistic, and no serious harm comes of them. Typically, two males in breeding condition will blacken their beards and perform head-bobbing behaviors, which are followed by a great bluff performance in which the males tilt their flattened bodies toward each other. One of the males may twitch its tail. One of them may then try to bite the other's tail. They may bob and again display their flattened bodies to each other. One of the males may then decide to latch on to the thick ridge of scales around the other male's neck in a movement that resembles breeding, pressing its body on top of the submissive animal. The beaten male then flattens on the ground. These behaviors help select for fitness in bearded dragons, allowing the largest, strongest, healthiest, and most spirited males first access to available females.

In captivity, especially in indoor enclosures, adult males can, and most certainly do, inflict some serious damage on each other, so it is important to keep males separately. The ideal situation is to keep the males from even seeing each other; otherwise, they can become stressed, even banging their faces against the enclosures in an attempt to reach their opponents. This stress is dangerous for the males, who can also stop eating, lose weight, and become so focused on another male that they forget breeding entirely.

TONGUE-TASTING

Bearded dragons taste new foods, new objects, other dragons, and new owners with their tongues. Tongue-tasting serves a chemoreceptive

The bearded dragon uses its tongue to learn about its surroundings.

function and allows evaluation and identification of food, objects, or other lizards. An alpha male may even tongue-taste another male prior to performing the head-bobbing display.

Tongue-tasting also gives the bearded dragon even more information than what is gathered by the "prongs" of its forked tongue. When the dragon retracts its tongue, these two prongs fit into the Jacobson's organ in the roof of the mouth, where taste and smell signals are sent to the brain as well as information to help the dragon better understand his environment.

EYE BULGING

Bearded dragons will bulge their eyes briefly, although no one is sure why. The most likely reason is that bearded dragons bulge their eyes when shedding to help shed the skin around and on their eyes. It is normal and not a problem. If their eyes swell or are closed for a period of time, this is a different situation. Consult Chapter 10 and, if necessary, see your veterinarian. Eye problems can be minimized by selecting a substrate other than sand.

CHAPTER 8

BREEDING BEARDED DRAGONS

Many people have set out to make money by breeding bearded dragons, hoping to meet the high demand for one of America's most popular pet reptiles. However, most of them go out of business, lasting only a couple of years because their projects lost money or were barely profitable.

Indoor space and setup, electricity, food, and maintenance costs can be surprisingly high when keeping large numbers of bearded dragons indoors. In warmer areas, outdoor setups such as greenhouses are more economical but can bring other problems, including fire ants and inclement or unpredictable weather.

As anyone who has made a living breeding amphibians and reptiles will tell you, it has to be a labor of love because it takes a great deal of work to make it in what many consider to be a cutthroat business. To be successful as a commercial breeder means doing research on the market, finding ready outlets for your animals, maintaining careful records of your breeding stock's performance, and carefully planning the expenses and expected returns.

Herpetoculture is a not only very competitive but also fast-changing. What is popular today may not be marketable a few years in the future, and what is rare today can become tomorrow's standard pet-trade fare, bred by every owner who cares to keep a pair together. To survive on a commercial level means constantly evaluating the market, the state and efficiency of your business, and your breeding stock. Ideally, you should always be looking to produce more vigorous, as well as more beautiful, dragons as economically as possible.

Breeding bearded dragons is a serious challenge. Let's say you've made up your mind and decide to go for it. Are you prepared for multiple clutches of eggs hatching within two weeks of each other? Where will you put all of those babies? If a typical clutch is twenty babies, and the female lays just three clutches, you are looking at housing, lighting, heating and feeding for sixty babies within about six weeks! Cleaning, misting, feeding twice a day, misting in the evenings, cleaning up, and caring for feeder insects can rapidly consume your life. Then you raise these sixty babies to 7-inch (18cm) size, and then what? If you crowd your babies, they will cannibalize each other—and how will you sell bearded dragons with missing limbs? And this example is just for one breeding pair!

Multiply the foregoing situation by however many pairs of dragons you have, and then add in the care of the parents. And don't forget about the babies you hold back because you love them too much to sell them. Those babies will need to be raised, fed, lit, and heated, too.

It is very easy to become completely overwhelmed. Do you want to take vacations? Spend time with friends? Have days off for national or religious holidays? Bearded dragons will eat and mess no matter what day it is. Do you have a job? Work late? Have a social life? Consider all of these points ahead of time. The reality of the situation is what causes most bearded dragon breeders to go out of business fast.

If you still think you are up to the challenge and personal sacrifice, read on. The following information will help you.

RECORD KEEPING

A key to the success of any commercial breeder is record keeping. This means, at the very least, giving each animal a number and documenting the parents of each clutch, the number of eggs laid by each female, and the number of eggs successfully hatched. Keeping digital records of individuals, labeled with their record number and including photos, allows you to easy access to your files when planning breeding projects. It saves time and allows a broader overview than examining individual animals in a collection.

Label egg clutches with their parentage and the date laid, and maintain accurate records of incubation temperature and duration. Often, bearded dragons are good producers for about three years before their numbers start declining significantly. Thus, replacing commercial breeding stock is an important way to optimize production;

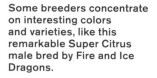

Some breeders concentrate on interesting colors and varieties, like this remarkable Super Citrus male bred by Fire and Ice Dragons.

Recording Your Finances

Carefully record your expenses and income for tax purposes and to allow you to hone the efficiency of your business.

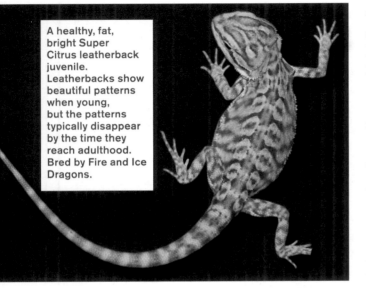

A healthy, fat, bright Super Citrus leatherback juvenile. Leatherbacks show beautiful patterns when young, but the patterns typically disappear by the time they reach adulthood. Bred by Fire and Ice Dragons.

this means planning ahead to raise replacement stock. If your goal is to develop your own unique lines or to maintain existing lines, careful record keeping will prove invaluable in identifying the best individuals for the process.

SELECTIVE BREEDING

Selective breeding is a term that refers to crossing animals with desirable traits to establish particular characteristics (such as color) in a line while maintaining vigor (size, health, and reproductive ability). Most of the attractive bearded dragon morphs available today were developed in this manner. Although inbreeding (breeding animals that are closely related, such as brother and sister or father and daughter) is a common and necessary component of selective breeding, it can decrease line vigor if practiced extensively over several generations. For this reason, selective breeding must also include outcrossing to other lines in order to reintroduce vigor from an unrelated gene pool while retaining the desirable trait(s).

The opposite of inbreeding, outcrossing refers to breeding animals with favorable traits to unrelated animals. Outcrossing not only adds line vigor but also can be used to introduce additional characteristics to a line. For example, German Giants were originally crossed with other lines of bearded dragons to increase size, reproductive vigor, and fecundity. Although first-generation offspring from an outcrossing may bear little resemblance to the brightly colored parent, breeding these outcrossed first-generation animals together will usually result in a percentage of offspring that manifest the desirable traits. You can then "fix" or intensify these traits through selective breeding.

When planning a breeding, it is important to ask yourself why. Why are you looking to breed a certain pair? Will this pair's offspring improve your line? Many breeders, especially new breeders, are myopic about color and forget the importance of vigor, size, and health. Too many bearded dragons grow up to be too small, which can be reflective of other problems, such as congenital defects. Granted, some of this is due to the quality of care that the bearded dragons received while growing up or to the health and genetic strength of the dragons originally purchased. As an example, some adult dragons barely reach 14 inches (36cm) in length. Responsible breeders would never breed a 14- or 15-inch (36- or 38cm) adult.

Hypo fire red translucent leatherback male with the black-eyed trait shown by some translucent dragons.

MAKE WISE CHOICES

As with breeders of any animal, bearded dragon breeders run the risk of becoming blind to their own lines. It is important to take an objective look at your breeding stock each year as you decide which animals to breed. What is good about this dragon? What would you like to improve? Then look at potential mates and assess them in the same way. For instance, breeders may choose to breed dragons that were average in color (but came from brilliantly colored parents) because they had the desired size, conformation, and vigor. Such a dragon can be paired with a brilliant dragon in the hopes that the offspring will have size and vigor as well as brilliant color. Generally speaking, babies will look like the parents and grandparents in terms of color alone (not counting hypomelanistic or translucent traits, which are recessive). So even if a dragon has average color, if its parents were vividly colored, there is a good chance that its offspring will achieve brilliant color.

As a breeder, you will raise many dragons that, as adults, will not meet your criteria. In those cases, you can sell them to families as pets. Although choosing which dragons to sell can be a difficult choice, it is impossible to keep every dragon. And the last thing you want to do is overcrowd the cages, which leads to illness and loss of breeding stock. By maintaining an objective view of your breeding stock and making the hard choices, your breeding stock will always improve.

Anyone can breed a male and female bearded dragon. However, producing quality dragons requires thought, planning,

Plan Ahead
When breeding, take the long view. Start with a five-year plan in terms of what you want to accomplish.

A hypo orange subadult male. Brilliant colors result from careful selective breeding.

and common sense. As a breeder, you must learn how to view dragons objectively to make smart breeding choices rather than just throwing any male and female together.

With that said, invest well in your breeding stock. It is better to have a few very high-quality bearded dragons than to have twenty dragons that are too small, of low vigor, and of mediocre color quality. However, it is not necessary to chase the latest trend. Make smart purchases and follow the advice given in this book.

BREEDING REQUIREMENTS

The first requirement for breeding bearded dragons is to have at least one healthy young adult male and one healthy young adult female. The second is to keep them together once they are about a year old and weight at least 350 grams. The third requirement, usually after the first breeding season, is to allow them a winter shutdown or brumation period. When they're mature, they will tend to brumate no matter what you do. In captivity, breeding starts after winter shutdown is over, beginning in the spring and often continuing into fall.

For bearded dragons being bred indoors, a 48-inch-long x 24-inch-deep (wide) x 18- or 24-inch-high (122 x 61 x 46 or 61cm) enclosure is the size most commonly used. As a breeder, you may have the most success keeping a pair together and having additional males in mind just in case. Some females can be very selective about which males and whose cage she likes best.

Other breeders find it is possible to keep trios of one male and two females with good breeding results. In larger enclosures, 72 x 30 inches (183 x 76cm) minimum, breeders have kept ratios of two males to four females and have found this to be effective for commercial-scale breeding. For commercial breeders, the expense of maintaining any more males than necessary can become cost prohibitive.

BREEDING PATTERNS

With bearded dragons raised under intensive rearing conditions, breeding begins as early as five to six months of age for males and can extend through the first winter. By twelve months of age, bearded dragons raised under intensive conditions may produce up to three clutches of eggs. During the course of their second year (twelve to twenty-four months old), they can lay up to eight clutches of eggs (two or three clutches before the first brumation period and four or five clutches after brumation).

Under less intensive rearing conditions in outdoor greenhouses and given a first-year brumation period, bearded dragons may not reach sexual maturity until they are twelve to fifteen months old. They will typically produce three clutches in their first eighteen months and up to seven clutches after the second (greenhouse conditions) brumation. The third year, they will produce only three or four clutches.

This is a pattern that is seen in several other species of quickly maturing lizards with high reproductive rates. The females are prolific breeders for the first two to three years and then steadily decline in production. By the age of six years, egg production is insignificant, and by seven years, it has often ceased completely. From the point of view of a commercial breeder, buying large adult captive-raised females is usually not the best investment.

Buying juvenile bearded dragons as potential breeders can be the best way to go. For one thing, you will know exactly how these animals have been cared for. Nothing is worse than spending good money on an adult only to find out the dragon requires expensive veterinary care and may not breed even after getting the required medical attention. In addition, it is very difficult for most potential new owners to gauge the age of adult bearded dragons. While you may think you are getting a two-year-old, it may actually be five.

This is not to say that adult dragons cannot be purchased in a healthy state. But, generally speaking, it is a far bigger risk to purchase an adult than a juvenile because the latter you can raise yourself with high-quality care.

Under normal indoor conditions, bearded dragons should not be bred too early. Males are ready sometimes by six months of age. However, that is too early for females. Breeding too early, even if she

Breeding and Brumation

As previously mentioned, beginning with their second winter, most bearded dragons in captivity undergo a period of shutdown called brumation. This period of brumation appears necessary for long-term success in breeding bearded dragons. As a rule, most mature bearded dragons shut down on their own, regardless of their living conditions, but a shift in environmental conditions also plays a role in initiating brumation.

successfully lays a clutch, usually results in small clutches, fewer clutches, and the potentially stunted growth of the female. If the male is also a first-time breeder, the female may lay many infertile eggs. With infertile eggs, there is a risk of egg-binding. For these reasons, some breeders only pair female bearded dragons that weigh at least 350 grams and are at least twelve months of age. Some breeders also do not raise males and females together because once the male becomes sexually mature, he can harass the female incessantly, which will stress her and can cause her to become ill. At the very least, she will likely lose weight.

If the female is ready (producing eggs), she will accept the male, performing the low bow to his head bobbing. If she is not ready to breed, she will scratch at the door of the enclosure, or, in a worst-case scenario, she may bite him. If she is not ready to breed, remove the female and let her be for a few weeks before trying again. In some cases, she just may not like that particular male. For this reason, it can be a good idea to keep "qualified" second males with desirable pedigrees in case she resists male #1. Some people say that if you have a great male, he will breed anything immediately. While this may sometimes be true, it does not seem to be the norm. Sometimes the girls just want the male they want, and that's the end of it.

COPULATION

About three to four weeks after the end of brumation, bearded dragons begin reproductive activities, including courtship, territorial and competitive behaviors, and copulation. In bearded dragons, copulation is typical of what is observed for most lizards. A male bites the fleshy portion of the nape of a female's neck, places part of his upper body on her, and then scratches her with his hind leg to encourage her to position herself for copulation. The male then twists his lower body and inserts a hemipenis. The sexual act lasts several minutes.

It is not unusual to see blood in the cage after copulation. As long as you do not see a prolapse from the male's vent, there is usually no need to worry.

Some males, especially a young male new to breeding, can do some damage to the female. Nasty bites on the neck, face, or even tail while he's trying to figure it out are common. On the other hand, some males never leave a mark on a female. Each male is different.

Note: Bearded dragon females have been known to hold sperm from one male to another (if moved). Because females can hold sperm for up to a year, a female may lay a clutch right after brumation even though she had been alone at the time. This can happen if the female holds sperm from a prior mating in the fall. This is yet another reason for keeping accurate records.

FROM GESTATION TO HATCHING

Gestation, the period between copulation and egg-laying, can be difficult to accurately determine in reptiles because females of many species can store sperm for extended periods of time. As a rule for bearded dragons, the interval between a first breeding and egg-laying will be about four to six weeks. Subsequently, the interval between clutches during a breeding season can vary depending on a number of factors; it could be as short as three weeks or considerably longer.

As the gestation period nears its end, the eggs pass through an area of the oviduct surrounded by the shell gland, which forms the calcareous shell. After they pass through the shell gland, you can often see the outlines of individual eggs (now more rigidly enclosed) pressing against the abdominal wall. They look like grapes or marbles.

Male and female bearded dragons.

Shortly afterward, the female lizard displays behaviors such as investigating possible laying sites and digging several test burrows. At this time, it is important to provide the gravid (pregnant) female with a nest site of at least 12 inches (31cm) of burrowing substrate. Most breeders provide horticultural vermiculite or damp soil as substrate. Substrate moisture is believed to provide important egg-laying cues regarding the suitability of the laying medium.

If the substrate is too shallow or causes the burrow to collapse repeatedly, the female may refuse to dig a nest and instead lay an egg a day on the surface until she finds a suitable laying site. This presents a problem because uncovered eggs have a high rate of dehydration and may be harmed by exposure to excess heat or sunlight. She may also dig several test holes and lay scattered eggs on the surface. She may eventually lay the rest of her eggs in shallow soil, but instead of digging her preferred nest (one deep enough that she can fit into completely, with just the tip of her snout showing out of the nest hole), she may lay them with the front of her body exposed.

An accessible 5-gallon (19L) plastic flower pot filled with moistened potting soil generally works well as a nesting site. After introducing the damp soil, compress it by pressing down on the soil surface with your hand. This makes the soil less likely to collapse as the female digs her nest. Alternatively, a nesting site can be made by placing soil at least 12 inches (31cm) deep at one end of the primary enclosure.

Another option is to place the female in a 30- or 55-gallon (114- or 208L) trash can with at least 12 inches (31cm) of soil in the bottom. Gently press down the moistened soil before introducing the female into the container.

After the female lays her clutch, she will usually be voracious, eating as much as she can. Many people have asked how many feeder insects they should allow a female to eat. Allow females to eat whatever they want to eat, in as large of quantities as they wish. Make sure that all foods are dusted with a calcium supplement.

Females are also often very thirsty after egg-laying. It is not uncommon to find a dragon that did not drink much before laying eggs suddenly drinking like a camel. She needs to replenish fluids lost in egg production. Instead of misting, soak the female every night and offer her water from a dripper first thing in the morning. Remember, a dehydrated dragon will not eat well, and you want the female to regain pre-laying weight as soon as possible; otherwise, her health can suffer.

CLUTCH SIZE

In inland bearded dragon collections, clutch sizes have ranged from as few as seven to as many as forty-six eggs, with most clutches ranging between twenty and thirty eggs. Back when German Giants were available, bearded dragons had been reported to lay in excess of fifty eggs per clutch, with a record of sixty-eight eggs. Clutch size varies depending on the sizes, ages, morphs, and lines of the parents. As a rule, younger, smaller females lay smaller clutches, and older females eventually lay smaller and fewer clutches. Being prepared for the maximum number of babies is preferable to the shock of having more babies than you can adequately house and feed.

INCUBATION

After your dragon lays her eggs, carefully dig through the soil, using your fingers or a tablespoon to expose the egg clutch. Next, transfer the eggs to an incubation container, such as a plastic storage box or an incubator containing 1½ inches (4cm) of incubating medium. The media most commonly used by breeders are coarse vermiculite, perlite, and a 50:50 mix of vermiculite and perlite. The original author was successful with only perlite by adding water to the medium until it felt moist but not soggy,

barely clumping in the hand but not dripping water when squeezed (this is about four parts incubating medium to three parts water by weight, not volume). Alternatively, you can use a mix of horticultural vermiculite (this is black like earth as opposed to silver rectangles), moistened until it holds a clump as previously described.

No matter which medium you use, bury the eggs halfway, horizontally, in the medium, leaving a small space between each egg. The eggs must be partially exposed to allow for monitoring and gas exchange. Also, if you are using a plastic container, pre-drill or punch holes around the top to allow for gas exchange, leaving at least 1½ inches (4cm) of air space between the top of the container and the eggs.

The ideal incubation temperature for bearded dragons is 82 to 85°F (28 to 29°C). To achieve this, most small-scale breeders use inexpensive poultry incubators, such as the HovaBator, or chick hatchers with no egg turner. Large-scale breeders construct heated cabinets using either light bulbs or heat tape controlled by a thermostat. Careful calibration is critical to prevent overheating.

Temperatures that are too warm (above 89°F [32°C]) will result in the death of the embryos, as will temperatures that are too cool (lower than 75°F [24°C] for long term or in the 60s Fahrenheit [about 16 to 21°C] or below for short term). Another important step is to check for hot and cool spots in the incubator. A thermometer and thermostatic control are essential to good monitoring.

It is also important to monitor moisture content in the substrate. Most breeders do this by picking up a clump of substrate, rolling it between their fingers, and pressing it into a ball. If the substrate still feels damp, it is probably fine. If it feels almost dry, then lightly moisten the substrate surface. Check the substrate weekly, but if you find it to be too dry, check it daily for a while and add drops of water as necessary.

Humidity within the incubator can be monitored as well. For a simple incubator (such as a HovaBator) with substrate placed directly on its floor, adding a small container of water helps maintain appropriate humidity levels. If using a thermostatically controlled incubator, there should be little condensation on the incubator's sides. However, if you are incubating eggs in a room with fluctuating day/night temperatures, there can be considerable condensation. This is not usually a problem if the substrate is appropriately moist. Adding ventilation holes to the sides of the egg container can reduce condensation but will dry out the substrate more quickly as well. If using pre-drilled plastic containers, remove excess condensation with a paper towel.

Incubation time varies according to species. Inland bearded dragon (*Pogona vitticeps*) eggs range from fifty-five to seventy-five days, depending on temperature. Eggs from Lawson's dragons (*P. henrylawsoni*) will hatch in forty-five to fifty-five days, and Eastern bearded dragon (*P. barbata*) eggs hatch in sixty-nine to seventy-nine days. With most clutches, all eggs will hatch within twenty-four hours of the first hatching, but some clutches may take as long as six days to fully hatch out.

The process of properly calibrating an incubator for the proper temperature can require several hours with homemade incubators or inexpensive poultry incubators. Calibrate the incubator at least twelve hours before introducing the eggs.

To calibrate an incubator, adjust the thermostat so that the temperature inside the incubator matches the desired setting. To get a temperature reading inside the incubator, place a mercury thermometer inside so it is visible through a window or install a digital thermometer with an external probe. Placing the probe inside the incubator and setting the switch to out/probe will give you a continuous readout as you adjust the thermostat. Because it takes time for the air temperature to equilibrate inside the incubator, you will need to make several thermostatic adjustments over a few hours for accurate calibration.

Note: It is important to keep the incubator in a room cooler than the desired incubation temperature, particularly during summer heat waves. Remember that an incubator heats but does not cool, so it cannot lower its temperature below the ambient air temperature. Placing the incubator in an air-conditioned room usually takes care of this problem. Brief exposure to high temperatures (above 90°F [32°C]) is more likely to kill a developing embryo than brief exposure to cooler temperatures.

If you live in a region that experiences frequent power outages, consider investing in a home generator to make sure that incubating eggs stay viable until the power returns. There is nothing as disappointing as going through the breeding process only to lose eggs in a power failure.

TURNING EGGS

Many herpetoculturists correctly warn against turning reptile eggs in the later stages of development. Lizard eggs begin to develop from the moment of fertilization, so development is usually well underway by the time the clutch is laid. At a certain stage in its development, the embryo forms an allantois, a membranous outgrowth from the midgut. This eventually expands and fuses with one of the membranes that encloses the embryo, called the chorion, to form the chorio-allantoic membrane, an area that allows gas exchange through the overlying shell.

Typically, the chorio-allantoic membrane forms at the top section of a resting egg with the back of the embryo curved beneath the allantois. Thus, in incubating eggs, the approximate position of the developing embryo is toward the top, close to where gas exchange readily occurs. Turning the egg in the later stages of development will shift the gas-exchange area and can cause compression, which, depending on the egg's position, may suffocate the embryo. So, the general rule is to avoid turning eggs once they have been placed in an incubator.

To keep a record of the original placement of the eggs, draw an X on top of each egg with a soft-lead pencil. In case of accidents or late discovery of eggs, you can "candle" them to determine embryo position. To do this, place a bright light behind a pinhole in a sheet of cardboard and view each egg with the light shining through it. The developing embryo will appear as a dark mass. Place the egg in the incubator so that the dark mass appears at the top.

HATCH FAILURE

Several factors can prevent eggs from hatching. When eggs show signs that they are going bad, the timing can indicate probable causes. First, check the incubation parameters, such as substrate moisture and temperature. If eggs incubated under proper conditions show early signs of collapse or molding, infertile

Assess the Eggs

A fertile egg looks like a marshmallow and will have a pink dot somewhere on it. If an egg is infertile, it will be yellowish with no pink dot. Just dispose of the infertile eggs and make sure to feed the female extra calcium, feeder insects, high-calcium greens, and vegetables to help her recover.

eggs are often the cause. You can verify this by slitting the collapsed eggs and checking for signs of early embryonic development and blood vessels. Factors that can cause the early demise of embryos include genetics and disease.

Late-stage death can be caused by genetic factors, improper temperatures or moisture levels, and possibly by faulty yolk composition. If incubation temperature is too high, there can come a point when the increased metabolism and higher oxygen requirements of late-stage embryos may exceed the amount of oxygen diffusing through the shell. At the first signs of late-stage egg death (collapse and no hatching within thirty-six hours), check the temperature and lower it a few degrees.

Another cause of hatching failure may be linked to temperatures that are too low and extend incubation for too long. Some lizard eggs incubated at relatively cool temperatures showed near-term hatchlings with soft bones and rubbery snouts and legs—signs of metabolic bone disease.

A current hypothesis is that incubation periods that extend too long can sometimes result in large hatchlings with depleted calcium reserves. Finally, it has been hypothesized that yolk compositions can be directly affected by the diet and supplements fed to the female, resulting in inadequate or excessive amounts of certain nutrients. These deficiencies or excesses may harm developing embryos, and this is a topic that deserves further study.

In many areas, carrion flies may infest bearded dragon eggs. These annoying pests take advantage of any deterioration or rupture of the shell to feed on the eggs' contents and lay their own eggs. They are readily attracted to the smell of eggs that have gone bad, so you should remove these eggs as soon you notice them. Otherwise, carrion flies will lay their eggs in the rotting dragon eggs, and, before long, your incubator will be

The baby dragons emerge from their shells.

Sex and the Single Bearded Dragon

Breeding responsibly requires a lot of time and space. Think long and hard before you decide to delve into breeding. Even if you decide that having just one bearded dragon is fine, you may still need to consider some facts of life.

One is that a female can retain sperm for up to one year. If you have a female, and she was housed with an adult male at any time, you may end up with eggs within the following year even if she is now housed singly. If you purchased a young female, and she has never been near a male, that still doesn't mean there will be no eggs. The eggs will be unfertilized, but there can still be eggs. Some females never produce eggs, while others may produce two or three unfertilized clutches a year. If this happens, you will have to supply a box and follow the same procedures mentioned earlier in this chapter, except you won't be incubating the eggs. Your female will still need some extra food and more calcium.

Females who have not been bred risk more of a chance of egg binding. That's when the eggs are formed, but she can't lay them. Egg binding can occur if heat and light are not adequate, or if there is no suitable place for the female to lay the eggs. If you think your dragon has eggs, make sure you are providing proper heat, light, and nutrition. If your female won't eat and is lethargic, and you can see or feel the eggs in her abdomen, giving her a nice soak in warm water may help the situation. If there's no immediate relief, get her to your veterinarian. Egg binding can be fatal.

Spaying your female is one way to prevent any problems, but there are risks. The odds of a dog or cat having serious complications or dying from spay/neuter is 1 percent. For a bearded dragon, it is 5 to 10 percent. Reptiles in general do not handle anesthesia well. Part of this is because they do not have a diaphragm, so they need help breathing during surgery. If you decide that you would like to spay your beardie, find a veterinarian who specializes in reptiles. That should increase the odds that your female will come through the surgery just fine.

When it comes to your male, especially after brumation, hormones are telling him it's time to mate. He may exhibit the head bobbing and beard displaying that a male does when there's a female nearby. Give him a sock or a stuffed toy instead, and he'll probably be quite happy.

infested with hundreds of these flies. If many carrion flies are in your incubator or the surrounding area, they will wait like predators for any opportunity to feed on animal matter, including a baby bearded dragon that has just slit its shell. In most cases, baby dragons will hatch before any real damage is done, but check for maggots in the umbilical area and in any remaining egg yolk. Rinse off any maggots with tap water.

HATCHING

For twenty-four hours prior to hatching, bearded dragon eggs sweat to varying degrees; the sweating is followed by a slight collapse and noticeable loss of turgidity twelve hours prior to hatching. Healthy, vigorous animals usually slit through the shell (using an egg tooth at the tip of the snout) within a few hours of this initial collapse. After hatching, newborn dragons may still be coated with albumin and will remain within the egg for several hours.

They should not be disturbed or removed from the incubation container until they have emerged from the eggs and show signs of activity. After the hatchlings are observed to be active, they can then be transferred to rearing containers. Knowing when to pull babies out comes with experience. Early hatching babies can trample and suffocate the later hatching siblings within a few hours. It is better to err on the side of caution and remove the babies the minute they are active. Some babies, though, will hatch with the yolk sac still attached. In this case, leave the baby in the vermiculite cup and in the incubator until the yolk sac is absorbed.

A closer look at a hatching dragon.

Do not handle or otherwise disturb a hatching baby.

CHAPTER 9

THE BOLD AND THE BEAUTIFUL: MORPHS

Part of the fun of owning reptiles is experiencing the variety in pattern and color produced by breeding. Whether the animals have special patterns or colors, the variants are usually referred to as "morphs." Perhaps nowhere are morphs more exciting and challenging than those in the bearded dragon world.

Inland bearded dragons have a wide distribution in Australia and consist of many populations adapted to specific habitats, ranging from sandy deserts to savannas, mountains, and woodlands. The variation found in these wild populations has allowed herpetoculturists to produce the range of morphs currently established in captivity.

According to Hauschild and Bosch (2000), the popular inland bearded dragons with high amounts of red originate from the central part of their range—an area characterized by red sands—while the more yellow specimens are found in the southern yellow-sand deserts. The availability of these more colorful desert morphs in the early 1990s allowed the selective breeding of many colorful varieties of bearded dragons available today.

HISTORY
NORMAL
The original brown and tan bearded dragons with small amounts of red and yellow, mostly on the head, were first imported into the United States in the late 1980s. "Normals" were the most readily available bearded dragons until the herpetocultural revolution generated imports of red/gold dragons in the 1990s. Because of the increased demand for more colorful dragons, most normal dragons in captivity have, over time, been crossed with other colors to the degree that it is becoming increasingly difficult to find representatives of the once common normal

The "normal" coloration was the most plentiful when bearded dragons became popular in the United States in the 1980s.

strain. This is the same herpetocultural trend seen in leopard geckos—selection for brighter colors and bolder patterns causes a decline in the pet trade of the original, normal-colored individuals.

GERMAN GIANT

Pete Weis introduced this morph into the United States hobby many years ago. German Giants were big dragons with aggressive personalities and were generally prolific breeders. They were colored mostly in browns and tans. The head was less massive than in typical dragons. The iris was a silvery gold that contrasted sharply with the pupil. Because of their high fecundity, German Giants had been crossed with other lines to increase reproductive vigor. The Giants, however, were a little more prone to aggressive behavior than are typical dragons. The early German Giants also diluted bright color in the lines, washing out the color.

Large males sometimes exceeded 24 inches (61cm) in length, and females had been known to lay a single clutch of more than fifty eggs, with a record of sixty-eight eggs. That said, it has been a many years since pure German Giants were available. While there are no purebred German Giants, many breeders do offer giant beardies if you like your dragons super-sized. Just remember that such a dragon will need more space and proportionately more food.

The red/gold coloration.

RED/GOLD

A great revolution in dragon breeding followed the importation of individuals with extensive amounts of reds and oranges and varying amounts of gold in the early 1990s. Originating in Germany, red/gold dragons allowed the selective breeding of the many orange, red, and yellow lines available today. The original German breeding stock was said to have come from the red deserts of the interior of Australia.

Additional imports of red/gold crosses between lines (e.g. normal x red/gold and Sandfire x red/gold) and selective breeding have allowed various breeders to develop their own unique lines. Because yellow and red pigments are synthesized by skin cells called xanthophores, the term "xanthic" may be the most appropriate to describe lines characterized by varying degrees of red or yellow coloration. Red/golds could be considered the most basic examples of xanthism that exist in bearded dragons.

MORPHS RECOGNIZED IN THE UNITED STATES

HYPERXANTHIC

Xanthic refers to the color yellow. A hyperxanthic beardie is one that, through selective breeding, has developed extensive saturation of red/orange or yellow (see photo at left).

TIGER

This was a line first introduced by Ron Tremper and is characterized by a barred pattern running the width of the body. Tiger-patterned dragons have cropped up here and there in certain breeders' citrus lines.

PARADOX

Paradox beardies have random patches of color, almost as if someone splattered paint on them. Sometimes these dragons are called "Purple Paradox" because the patches of color are often blue or purple, but the patches can be any color.

WITBLITS

This is a more recent patternless mutation. These dragons are usually a pale, sandy orange.

A citrus tiger dragon.

STRIPED

The Dunner, a striped dragon produced by Kevin Dunne, is a more recent variety of striped bearded

This dragon exhibits the translucent trait as well as the Dunner striped pattern.

A Witblits morph.

dragon. The scales on a Dunner grow in multiple directions: on the beard, the spikes point outward rather than downward.

HYPOMELANISTIC (HYPO)

These are dragons in which the dark pigmentation (melanin) is greatly reduced or nearly absent. Although some are very bleached in appearance, they are not true albinos because their eyes remain pigmented (in true albinism, eyes are pink or orange/red). One of the characteristics of hypomelanistic dragons is a clear-colored nail base. Hypomelanistic bearded dragons include hypo pastels, which can have a light bluish to purplish body pattern, probably caused by clear skin areas that expose underlying iridophores, which are skin pigment cells that underlie xanthophores and have the ability to reflect light of a specific wavelength.

LEUCISTIC

This morph was originally a gray/white dragon with dark eyes. It was misnamed, however, as true leucistic animals have blue eyes. It has since disappeared into other white lines.

A hypomelanistic translucent striped dragon. Hypomelanism reduces the pigmentation of the base color.

A "hypo" dragon appears less vivid in color but still has dark eyes.

ZERO

As beautiful as they are, this is arguably the most difficult color morph to produce. Zero dragons are another type of patternless dragon, like the Witblits. The color of zero dragons ranges from off-white to silver-gray. Whites seem to be difficult to produce, as they usually lay fewer clutches with fewer eggs.

A hypo fire red juvenile.

GREEN

There is at least one natural population of gray-green bearded dragons in Australia. In captivity, a pale green line was developed through selective breeding in England, but it has been difficult to maintain and therefore is not commonly available in the pet trade.

GOLD IRIS

This trait of unusually light, bright, silvery gold irises crops up in many breeders' lines.

TRANSLUCENT/BLACK EYES

Some say that translucent dragons originated in Belgium. It is not unusual to see bearded dragons with a new trait pop up all over the world from different breeders at around the same time.

This mutation is described by its name: this type of dragon has somewhat translucent skin as opposed to the opaque of "normal" bearded dragons. This is especially noticeable when the dragons are young. Typically, this morph is combined with black eyes. It is a recessive trait.

LEATHERBACK

This mutation displays reduced tubercles (the raised scales, or spikes, on the dragons' skin). Originally there were two variations—the Italian and the American—but because of cross-breeding, pure lines are not commonly found. The leatherback mutation is a codominant trait.

SILKBACK

The breeding of two leatherback bearded dragons produces silkback offspring. While leatherback bearded dragons have reduced tubercles, silkbacks have none; the skin of the silkback is very delicate and completely smooth. These dragons require additional attention, such as regular application of special moisturizers to keep the skin from splitting. There is a moral argument as to whether or not these dragons should be produced. Some people love silkbacks, while others dislike their look.

The rare zero dragon is very pale with no pattern.

A hypo leatherback dragon.

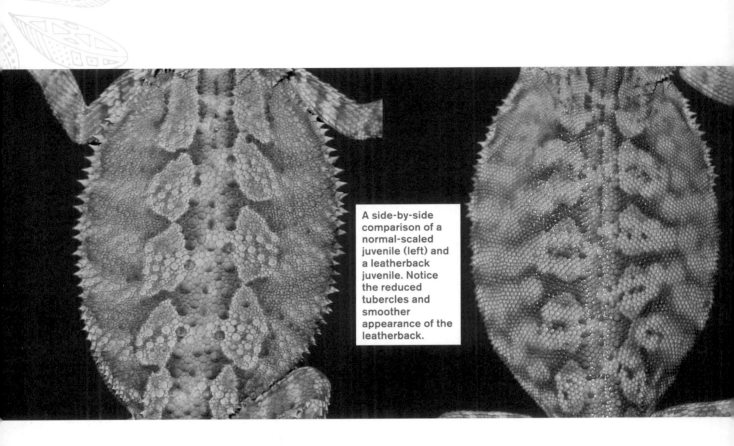

A side-by-side comparison of a normal-scaled juvenile (left) and a leatherback juvenile. Notice the reduced tubercles and smoother appearance of the leatherback.

UNDERSTANDING BEARDED DRAGON GENETICS

The term "phenotype" refers to the visual color and mutations displayed in the dragon. The term "genotype" refers to the underlying genetics and any recessive traits that the dragon carries but does not display. An example of this is hypomelanism, a recessive trait. In simplest terms, if your dragon displays clear nails, it is a "hypo" (hypomelanistic) dragon. If your dragon does not display the clear-nailed trait, it may still carry this recessive gene, which it inherited from one of its parents. If a parent carries the hypo gene, the offspring will be heterozygous (or "het") for hypomelanism. A recessive trait is displayed only when both parents carry that trait. **Note:** "Normal" nails are dark nails and important for the following explanation.

If you breed:

- Hypo to normal (dark-nailed): 100 percent of the offspring will be het for hypo
- Hypo to hypo: 100 percent of the offspring will be hypo

- Hypo to het hypo: 50 percent of the offspring will be hypo and 50 percent will be het hypo
- Het hypo to het hypo: 50 percent of the offspring will be het hypo, 25 percent will be hypo, and 25 percent will have normal (dark) nails; 66 percent are possible hets
- Het hypo to normal: 50 percent of the offspring will be het hypo and 50 percent will have normal nails; 50 percent are possible hets

In the foregoing explanation, *hypo* can be replaced with *translucent* because the translucent gene is also recessive.

Some mutations pop up with little explanation. This makes breeding bearded dragons truly exciting!

THE FUTURE

Bearded dragons are becoming one of the most popular pet reptiles of all time, so it should be no surprise that there is an active interest in developing new, attractive, and marketable lines of this species. As with certain kinds of fish, such as koi carp and goldfish, or with lizards, such as the popular leopard gecko, there will be many more attractive and unusual morphs of bearded dragons in the future.

Normal (dark) nails on a 100-percent citrus dragon (top); clear nails on a hypo Super Citrus dragon.

CHAPTER 10

DISEASES OF BEARDED DRAGONS AND THEIR TREATMENTS

When bearded dragons were first introduced as a new type of reptile pet, it appeared that it was a truly bulletproof lizard. Bearded dragons were hardy, good eaters, and easy to care for. Health problems were rare, and most disorders were chalked up to glitches in evolving husbandry techniques. As always happens with new reptiles, fanciers' knowledge about bearded dragons expanded exponentially as the species became more popular.

However, bearded dragons are not perfect. While quite hardy, these lizards are afflicted by various ailments. Medical and surgical knowledge of bearded dragons is increasing, but customer demand is what drives the evolution of new medical information and techniques. Much of what is medically applied to the bearded dragon is information borrowed from research on the green iguana. More species-specific information is needed, which is where you, the bearded dragon owner, can help. Participation and contribution to research at your local herpetological society or with the Association of Reptile and Amphibian Veterinarians is critical for the development of new medical information and techniques.

RECOGNIZING SICK BEARDED DRAGONS

One reason bearded dragons have become so popular is that they are personable and animated. Unlike certain snakes, which spend a considerable amount of time wrapped up and relaxing contentedly, bearded dragons are active and entertaining. Each dragon has a unique personality and unique behavioral patterns, which are important for owners to notice and evaluate during their normal caretaking duties.

Simply put, sick children look sick, sick dogs look sick, sick cats look sick—and sick bearded dragons look sick. They act sick, too. If, as an owner of a bearded dragon, you have missed the foot-stomping, arm-waving, tail-swishing, head-bobbing, sideways head-tilting, and various other gymnastic techniques that bearded dragons use to communicate their feelings, resolve to watch more carefully in the future.

The most common signs of a sick bearded dragon are listlessness, inactivity, lying flat (instead of raising the body when standing), failing to eat or drink, and lack of normal communicative body language. In short, they are depressed and won't eat. Do any of these actions, or the lack thereof, indicate a particular disease or ailment? Unfortunately, they do not. These symptoms can be noted in all of the serious yet common bearded dragon ailments discussed here.

Often, bearded dragons do not show many signs of illness until they are critically ill. For this reason and perhaps lack of good routine observation habits, bearded dragons can look fine one day and be gravely ill the next. The bearded dragon in your care relies on you, the owner, to watch for any signs that things are not quite as they should be. Weighing your beardie each week is a good way to stay alert to any changes in health. If you see a sudden drop of 15–20 grams in a week, check for the other previously mentioned signs. Examine the stools. Are they normal, or do they have a particularly bad odor? Is the dragon eating normally or has its appetite dropped off? Is it lying down or standing alert? Any of these symptoms in conjunction with sudden weight loss should trigger a visit to the vet.

A healthy bearded dragon is alert and enjoys its usual activities, such as basking.

PARASITES
COCCIDIA

Coccidiosis is the most common disorder seen in bearded dragons. Coccidia are microscopic protozoan parasites that live primarily in the small intestine and replicate in the lining cells of the intestinal tract. The end product of the reproductive process are microscopic

Proper hydration and moisture in the enclosure contribute to the dragon's overall well-being.

entities called oocysts. These tiny oocysts are passed into the environment with the feces when the bearded dragon has a bowel movement. The oocysts can then reinfect the host by being ingested.

This can happen in many ways. Your dragon may walk through his own waste, then contaminate his food or water with oocysts as he goes. Feeder insects in the cage may also come in contact with the contaminated feces. Your beardie may even nibble his stool, which is not abnormal behavior for a bearded dragon. This is a direct life cycle at work; no intermediate hosts are required. One coccidium becomes a dozen, twelve coccidia become hundreds, and so on.

It could be that, in the wild, bearded dragons can move away from their stools, and they certainly are not enclosed with feeder insects; therefore, they do not contaminate themselves. But bearded dragons housed in captivity in enclosures do not have that luxury. In any case, regardless of the source, coccidia should be eliminated whenever possible for the following reasons:

- The parasites have a direct life cycle and build up to tremendous levels in captive animals. This is known as a superinfection.

Did You Know?
Coccidia are so prevalent in bearded dragons that they have their own species—*Isospora amphiboluri.*

- Coccidia invade the cells of the intestinal lining to reproduce. In large numbers, this can lead to gastrointestinal pain, diarrhea, malabsorption, and fluid loss—and eventually to a failure to eat, weight loss, secondary nutritional disorders, and secondary bacterial infections.
- Hatchling bearded dragons appear to pick up coccidia even when not exposed to the parents' environment, which implies transuterine or egg-related transfer. At some point, this cycle must be broken.
- The coccidia may be transmissible to other reptiles. While coccidia are somewhat host-specific, there have been no studies to determine whether *I. amphiboluri* affects other reptiles.

So how to get rid of coccidia? It's not easy, and it's not fun. For years, sulfa drugs such as sulfadimethoxine (Albon) and trimethoprim-sulfa (multiple manufacturers) were standard for eliminating coccidia in bearded dragons. However, sulfa drugs take a toll on a bearded dragon's body, and now a common treatment is Ponazuril, a coccidiocide. Obtain medication from your veterinarian after a coccidia diagnosis is confirmed via a fecal examination, and give your beardie the medicine on the schedule instructed by your vet.

The secret to eliminating this disease resides in environmental control. You have to become an obsessive cage cleaner; if you already are, that's even better. To have a chance at breaking the coccidia exposure cycle, you must reduce the cage to the bare essentials. Maintain the use of heat lamps. Use newspaper or paper towels on the floor of the cage and change it at least once or twice daily. Don't try to clean branches and rocks with cracks, crevices, or holes; instead, throw them out. Use cardboard cage furniture, such as egg cartons, that you can get rid of daily. Offer water in simple dishes and clean the dishes thoroughly twice every day.

Discard uneaten feeder crickets, superworms, waxworms, or veggies anywhere from thirty minutes to twenty-four hours after feeding. Do not recycle them or save them to use with other reptiles. Remember,

A Word of Warning

Medication should be used only if coccidia have been diagnosed, which is typically done through a fecal flotation. Sulfa drugs used to be the most common drugs prescribed for eliminating coccidia, but they are potentially dangerous to dehydrated reptiles and have been replaced by safer options. Rely on your reptile veterinarian for diagnosis, prescription of medications, and follow-up fecal examinations.

the insects may have dined on dragon droppings and would only serve to perpetuate the cycle.

Herpetologist Dr. Richard Funk prefers having side-by-side cage setups in which one cage is always clean. Simply switch the bearded dragon to the other cage and then clean the one from which you removed the lizard. Switch as often as necessary to decrease the possibility of exposure to fecal material and, therefore, coccidia oocysts. Sound like a pain? It is! It will often take up to six weeks for treatment to be successful.

Even then, run a follow-up fecal exam

Scrupulous cleanliness of the enclosure, the substrate, and all accessories is necessary for disease prevention and control.

two to three weeks after stopping the treatment protocol. Make sure your lizards are coccidia-free before mixing and matching dragons. The good news is that once a group is clean, the dragons will stay clean unless new coccidia-bearing dragons are introduced.

Treating a large group of bearded dragons in such a manner is obviously difficult, if not impossible. This regimen is a nuisance to practice for two lizards, much less two hundred, so you can see how hard it can be for breeders to eliminate coccidia. However, studies are always being conducted on reliable parasite-eradication protocols, offering true hope that coccidia will someday be a thing of the past.

Remember the importance of quarantining new animals. A group of bearded dragons can become reinfected by the premature addition of a new arrival. New dragons should be isolated for at least a few weeks and have fecal tests run on at least three samples over the same time period before being determined parasite-free.

Ask your veterinarian if they recommend supportive care in the form of reptile probiotics or electrolytes if your dragon is taking medication for coccidia. Fortunately, Ponazuril, a common prescription for coccidia, is not harsh on the bearded dragon's system.

PINWORMS

Pinworms are another group of parasites that are ubiquitous in bearded dragons. While considerably less harmful than coccidia, pinworms can reach tremendous parasitic loads due to their direct life cycles.

Pinworms are diagnosed via fecal examination, and they are easily eliminated by administering oral fenbendazole (Panacur). A common recommendation is a daily dose for three to five days, and then repeating this regimen ten days later. Follow-up fecals should be run three weeks after the last treatment.

MICROSPORIDIA

Dr. Elliott Jacobson reported the first cases of this intracellular protozoan parasite in three bearded dragons that had been inappetent and depressed and that eventually succumbed to the protozoan parasites. While known to infect some amphibians and other reptiles, microsporidia had not been previously reported in bearded dragons.

These obligate intracellular unicellular protozoans are important pathogens of invertebrates. It has been speculated that feeder insects were the source of infection, which is unlikely. The main source of transmission is probably spores shed from infected reptiles. While uncommon, this is a parasite that reptile veterinarians watch out for. It possesses characteristics that reptile owners and veterinarians dislike—a direct life cycle and resistant spores that can persist up to a year in the environment.

TAPEWORMS

While not diagnosed as frequently as other parasites, tapeworms may be more common in bearded dragons than is typically recognized. Possible tapeworm infection should be considered in bearded dragons that have been treated for coccidia and pinworms yet are not gaining weight despite ravenous appetites. An analogous situation was seen in ball pythons that had trouble gaining weight despite

Illustration of adult pinworms in the colon.

good appetites and appearing otherwise healthy. Occasionally, these animals have been treated for tapeworms despite no definitive proof of their presence. Such a course of treatment should be based on discussions with your reptile veterinarian, who knows the overall health parameters of the bearded dragon in question.

A tapeworm segment, or proglottid, resembles a grain of rice and can be seen in the feces.

The most common means of diagnosing tapeworms is by the presence of tapeworm segments (proglottids) in the feces. Proglottids are small, white, rice-shaped segments that can be found on the surface of the feces or moving away from it. These segments contain tapeworm eggs to be distributed to the environment either by desiccation of the segment (thereby releasing the eggs) or by being ingested. Tapeworm eggs can be found on routine fecal flotations but seem to be present only in very heavy infestations. Treatment consists of either an oral or injectable dose of praziquantel (Droncit), which is repeated after two weeks.

Tapeworms require intermediate hosts and have indirect life cycles, so self-exposure is not the problem it is with coccidia or pinworms.

PENTASTOMIDS

Pentastomids are relatively rare, but a book on bearded dragons and frilled lizards written by Hauschild and Bosch (2000) stated that necropsies performed on ninety-three bearded dragons had yielded eleven with pentastomids.

Pentastomids have an indirect life cycle, requiring intermediate hosts such as insects and rodents to complete their reproductive cycle. Extensive larval migration occurs before adults form in the lungs and complete the cycle by laying eggs that are then passed through the feces and into the environment. Despite large numbers and extensive larval migration of these prehistoric caterpillar-like parasites, most infestations occur without major symptoms. In some cases, there can be damage to the tissue during larval migration or when adults are in the lungs.

Treatment to date has been with ivermectin, which has thus far been found to reduce the number of ova passed but not to stop the shedding altogether. Pentastomids pose an unknown zoonotic risk, and owners should be informed of this if their bearded dragons are affected. This is not a parasite to take home to Mom.

MITES

Mites are uncommon external parasites and do not appear to be indigenous to bearded dragons; when they do appear, they seem to be acquired from other reptiles within a collection. Snake mites will infest bearded dragons and can be seen crawling on the lizards with the naked eye.

As with all mite infestations, the environment plays a critical role in treatment. Change the substrate to newspaper, at least temporarily, to eliminate spots where the mites can hide and breed. Change the paper substrate at least two to three times a week. Reduce cage furniture to a minimum and eliminate all rocks or branches with cracks and crevices. An initial cage cleaning with a mix of water and bleach (one capful of bleach to each gallon of water) helps to mechanically eliminate mites and their eggs.

One way to treat mites is to use an ivermectin-based spray (5–10 milligrams of ivermectin per quart of tap water). Remove the lizard and water dish from the cage and spray the entire enclosure with this solution after a thorough cleaning. Once the cage is dry, gently but thoroughly spray the lizard, including the face and eyes, with the solution and then return it to its cage. Once the lizard is completely dry, put the water dish back in the cage. Repeat this protocol every four to five days for three weeks.

It's important to note that ivermectin is not a quick-kill product, so you may continue to see mites moving for the first few days of treatment. Store the spray in a dark cabinet between treatments and mix a new batch every thirty days.

Mites can be challenging to control in outdoor enclosures due to the numerous

Outdoor enclosures provide plenty of hiding spots for pesky parasites.

hiding spaces and other variables. For large outdoor enclosures, move the lizards to smaller indoor cages for individual treatment with the aforementioned ivermectin spray and treating the outdoor enclosures with a pyrethroid (type of insecticide) product designed for flea control in dogs and cats. The lizards should remain off the sprayed area until it has completely dried, and it is ideal to keep the lizards in indoor cages for the entire course of treatment—about three weeks. If you must return them to the outdoor enclosures, wait until the sprayed areas are completely dry. Most of the toxicity of pyrethroids has been linked to respiratory exposure in nonventilated containers, so a pyrethroid spray used as instructed in an open-air enclosure should be relatively safe, as long as the lizards are not present when the product is sprayed, as inhaling the spray can be lethal to them. Pyrethroids have residual action and, depending on the product, need only be applied every one to three weeks. Spray the dragons with the ivermectin mixture every four to five days for three weeks.

CALCIUM DEFICIENCY

One of the great benefits of being a reptile owner is that you get to observe feeding behaviors. Bearded dragons are just plain cool to feed. A healthy, hungry bearded dragon will perform an Olympic-quality floor exercise while polishing off a dozen crickets, mealworms, or waxworms. It is so much fun to feed insects to bearded dragons that sometimes people feed them insects only. And, as often as not, the dragons

Alert behavior and normal appetite are signs that a bearded dragon is in good health.

are so satisfied with their crickets that they refuse to eat vegetable matter. However, MacMillen, Augee, and Ellis (1989) have reported that, in the wild, vegetable matter makes up as much as 90 percent and 50 percent of the diets for adult and juvenile bearded dragons, respectively.

There are benefits to having fresh veggies available daily:

• Greens and veggies are important sources of fiber, vitamins, and other nutrients.
• The availability of produce reduces intraspecies mutilations.
• Crickets and other invertebrate prey can gutload on the salad prior to being eaten.
• Reducing the overall dietary protein and fat while increasing vegetable intake may extend longevity.

Keep in mind, though, that even when greens and veggies are fed along with crickets and other insects, nutritional disorders may occur. The most common nutritional disorder I've seen in bearded dragons is calcium deficiency in the form of hypocalcemia (low blood calcium), the most common cause of which is a diet of almost exclusively crickets.

Most feeder crickets come straight from a pet store and have not been fed balanced diets (gutloaded) or dusted with nutritional supplements prior to being fed to dragons. Calcium deficiency is also seen in bearded dragons fed excessive amounts of meat products because these diets are low in calcium, and less calcium in the dragon's body leads to stimulation of receptors in the parathyroid gland, which in turn causes the release of parathyroid hormone (PTH). Increased levels of PTH activate bone cells (osteoclasts) to start demineralizing bone to release calcium into the bloodstream.

If the primary problem presents as soft bones and multiple fractures, the dragon's disease is termed metabolic bone disease (MBD). MBD is displayed in distorted backs, paralyzed back legs, and other bone deformities. If the primary problem is twitching and seizures, then the dragon likely suffers from hypocalcemia (which is more common in juvenile dragons).

The other main source of calcium deficiency is vitamin D_3 deficiency, or hypovitaminosis D. This fat-soluble vitamin is essential to the uptake and

This bearded dragon really gets into his greens.

utilization of calcium in the body. Bearded dragons produce much of their vitamin D_3 from the reaction of UV light on their skin. This converts a cholesterol-derived product from previtamin D to active vitamin D_3. The synthesis doesn't occur in dragons housed indoors without exposure to UVB. (See Chapter 4 for information on UVB, sunlight, and UVB-emitting bulbs.)

SIGNS OF CALCIUM DEFICIENCY

Muscles require calcium to contract properly. Calcium deficiency leads to muscle pain and dysfunction, such as when the smooth muscle of the gastrointestinal tract won't support peristaltic waves, resulting in constipation.

Sometimes, the first signs seen in young calcium-deficient dragons are bloating and constipation. When a dragon has a low calcium level for an extended period of time, muscle tremors set in. Toes and feet begin to twitch. These symptoms call for immediate calcium supplementation. As a bone is demineralized by the PTH-driven osteoclasts, the bony matrix is fortified with fibrous tissue (termed "fibrous osteodystrophy"), resulting in a brittle, swollen, and painful bone.

Calcium-deficient dragons initially look like any sick bearded dragons—weak, depressed, and reluctant to move. Very young dragons may be tremendously bloated and uncomfortable. Occasionally, twitching of toes and limbs is noted prior to handling, but sometimes twitching won't become evident until the lizard is stressed by handling. Twitching (hypocalcemic tetany) appears in bearded dragons prior to extensive bony changes, such as swollen limbs and softened jaws (rubber jaw). This is in contrast to green iguanas and other lizards, which may suffer extensive damage prior to muscle tetany.

TREATMENT

Bearded dragons with signs of calcium deficiency should be treated right away with calcium supplementation. Neo-Calglucon, an oral product for humans, is a good first source of calcium because it seems to be better absorbed than other products. Next, review the lizard's diet and your husbandry methods to see if a vitamin D_3 injection is justified. Constipated animals are given gentle enemas or have their bowels emptied mechanically. Supportive care in the form of fluids and involuntary feeding is employed until a dragon is well enough to start eating its corrected diet.

> ### MBD and Diet
> Early-state MBD may be reversed with a diet of black soldier fly larvae and greens for about two months. The reason for this is that the larvae are very high in calcium. While this is no substitute for veterinary care, it is something to consider.

Your vet will determine whether calcium injections are needed or if you can supplement your dragon at home.

Some dragons are so weak that attempting oral calcium, fluids, or foodstuffs could easily result in aspiration pneumonia. Even the most debilitated lizard can have a pharyngostomy tube (placed by a qualified veterinarian), through which you can give medications, fluids, and food.

Each bearded dragon has its own specific needs. For example, if you have three enclosures with one bearded dragon in each, and you give all three the same amount of calcium supplementation and they are all on UVB, they may not all absorb calcium at the same rate. In other words, two could be fine, with the other one showing signs of deficiency.

It is also a good idea to make sure that your UVB fluorescent tube is still providing UVB in the therapeutic range. If your UVB bulb is a year old, it obviously will not be as therapeutic as a new bulb. It is wise to invest in a UVB meter to stay on top of the UVB output.

PREVENTION

As with most diseases, calcium deficiency is best prevented rather than treated. The reader should review the sections in this book on husbandry and diet as well as the strategies emphasized here.

It is essential to expose young bearded dragons to a wide variety of vegetable matter so that they get used to eating these foods and consume them as part of their usual diet. Some young bearded dragons enjoy the vegetable varieties of baby food for humans, into which you can stir small quantities of calcium.

For calcium supplementation, it used to be that calcium carbonate (no phosphorus or vitamin D_3), was obtained from health-food stores or in the form of Tums antacid tablets. Owners would dust crickets or invertebrates two or three times a week for young, growing dragons.

Now, there is a range of calcium products available, such as Repti Calcium, Rep-Cal®, and Repashy SuperCal. Hatchlings, juveniles, young subadults, and breeding pairs should be given this supplement daily at one feeding.

The UVB bulb will allow the dragon to absorb the calcium supplement. Place the bulb on the enclosure's top within 12 inches (31cm) of the dragons and leave it on for twelve to fifteen hours in the summer and for ten to twelve hours in the spring and fall. Select the bulb carefully, because only a few on the market produce significant levels of UVB. Zoo Med, Arcadia, and other such companies make excellent products for this purpose. Replace the bulb every six to nine months to ensure adequate UVB production.

Don't go overboard, though. More is not necessarily better. Vitamin D toxicity is a real concern because it can easily be acquired through the use of products containing high levels of vitamin D_3 at every dusting. Calcium has one of the most narrow safety margins of all nutrients and can produce signs of disease when fed in excessive amounts. Offer vitamin supplements, such as Herptivite, one to three times a week, depending on the age of the dragon.

ADENOVIRUSES IN BEARDED DRAGONS

Adenovirus disease in bearded dragons is poorly understood for the same reason most reptile diseases are inadequately delineated—lack of funding for critical research. Here's what is known.

A variety of greens and veggies contributes to overall nutritional balance.

Unfortunately, there are no specific signs to watch for in bearded dragons sick with adenovirus. Most of the bearded dragons that have been diagnosed with adenovirus have had a history of failing to thrive, sometimes showing poor appetite or sometimes exhibiting diarrhea. Sometimes they die. The young, especially those four to twelve weeks old, appear to be affected more often than older specimens. Rather vague, wouldn't you say?

An affected animal is typically difficult to differentiate from one with coccidiosis or certain forms of calcium deficiency.

To further complicate matters, dragons can have multiple disorders. A young bearded dragon with adenovirus could also have coccidiosis, which may or may not be causing problems at that moment. This young dragon could, or would, certainly develop nutritional disorders, including hypocalcemia, because poor food intake becomes a factor. These mix-and-match illnesses could go on and on, with one factor affecting another or making no difference.

It's important to know if adenovirus is present in a sick dragon. Laboratory testing is available to determine a dragon's adenovirus status.

So, do all bearded dragons that test positive for adenoviruses die? No. In fact, many can live somewhat normal lives. Some become chronic "poor doers" that come around slowly but can eventually recover, or at least appear to recover. Supportive care techniques—including force-feeding, fluids, and occasionally administering antibiotics for secondary infections—increase their survival rate.

It is suspected that an adenovirus-positive bearded dragon can carry and shed the virus for the rest of its life. It is also suspected that the virus is given from one sick reptile to another through fecal and oral,

Any disease that is shed in the feces poses a risk of transmission between dragons kept together.

or even airborne, exposure. Whether you have a small group of pets or a large breeding colony, a virus severely complicates things. While there is always the risk of death, there is also the risk of spreading the disease by selling or trading the original lizards or their offspring. In essence, a diagnosis of adenovirus within a group of dragons should make them a closed group, with no additions to or subtractions from the infected group.

OTHER HEALTH CONCERNS
KIDNEY DISEASE AND GOUT

Water is extremely important to the elimination of nitrogenous waste products in all reptiles. Because bearded dragons originate in the red sand deserts of Australia, it was assumed that bearded dragons have durable kidneys. Most desert-dwelling reptiles have adapted to extremely dry conditions by developing mechanisms to preserve water and to excrete concentrated uric acid.

Apparently, the methods employed by bearded dragons have not yet been discovered or appreciated, because evidence of renal disease is on the rise. Hauschild and Bosch (2000) stated that a group of necropsies on ninety-three bearded dragons revealed that 30 percent of the specimens had primary and secondary visceral gout.

First, a very brief review of gout. As mentioned previously, the nitrogenous waste product that bearded dragons must eliminate from their blood stream is uric acid, which is a highly insoluble product. If the kidneys become damaged by age, drugs, and chronic dehydration, they will be unable to properly filter out uric acid, which will increase in the bloodstream.

If the resulting condition, called hyperuricemia, becomes extreme, uric acid crystals are deposited into internal organs, causing severe inflammation and sometimes organ failure. The deposit of uric acid into tissues is often referred to as gout, and when it involves the internal organs, it is called visceral gout. Deposition of uric acid due to kidney damage is termed primary visceral gout. If the kidneys are not damaged initially, and dehydration leads to the hyperuricemia and deposits of uric acid, it is referred to as secondary visceral gout.

Visceral gout is usually fatal in bearded dragons unless corrected very early in its course. Some experts have speculated that wild bearded dragons retreat to moist underground burrows or stay buried to prevent the loss of fluids. In the wild, adult bearded dragons appear to eat mainly vegetation, which can be a major source of moisture. It is hoped that husbandry factors, such as excessively dry substrates, basking under a heat lamp, and a lack of moist veggies are the cause of

dehydration, because these can easily be corrected. Kidney failure due to excessive calcium and vitamin D_3 administration is common in other lizards, particularly the green iguana. The presence of excessive D_3 leads to the uptake of excessive calcium and subsequent mineralization of the kidneys. With luck, further research on this topic will find some simple husbandry practices to help maintain captive specimens with normal kidneys. If diagnosed early, treatment centered around fluid therapy can be initiated and husbandry practices reviewed.

PROLAPSES

Prolapses are not common in bearded dragons, but they do occur, and they should be treated as a relative emergency. The most common type seen in practice is hemiperal prolapse after breeding. The prolapsed hemipenis is a relatively large (¾ inch long by ¼ inch wide [6mm x 1.9cm]) bright-red to dark-red mass protruding from the vent of the affected male. The treatment is to gently clean and lubricate the tissue and then gently push it back into the vent with a lubricated cotton swab.

The problem is that by the time this problem is noticed, the tissue is often quite inflamed and swollen and cannot be replaced without it popping back out. If the tissue becomes excessively swollen, begins to dry out, or is traumatized by being dragged around the cage, the hemipenes' vascular supply could become damaged, necessitating an eventual amputation.

Because so many variables exist with prolapses, the ideal course of action is to have your reptile veterinarian examine the dragon right away. The veterinarian can evaluate the tissue for viability and use sutures to help the hemipenes stay in place.

Another important consideration is that some prolapses are of rectal tissue, which may be much more difficult to identify. These prolapses are even more important to handle promptly and correctly. A bearded dragon can live without a hemipenis, but it can't live without a functional rectum.

Without proper lighting, the dragon's immune system will not function at its best.

Rectal prolapses often result from chronic straining, so any dragon who is straining to defecate should be evaluated for internal parasites, gastrointestinal infections, constipation, gastrointestinal obstructions, and, in females, egg-binding. In addition, rectal prolapses can recur if their underlying cause is not identified and corrected.

EGG-BINDING

Review the Chapter 8 if there is any chance your female dragon could be gravid (or pregnant). A basic understanding of the bearded dragon reproductive cycle is helpful when dealing with problems. A gravid female is usually easy to detect because her abdomen is swollen and her body weight has increased. She looks pregnant. If the dragon crawls across your open palm with your fingers slightly elevated, you can often feel the grape-sized eggs in her lower abdomen.

Behaviorally, pregnant dragons often continually dig and squat and then move to a new spot and try again. They are agitated and tired, and they usually won't eat properly due to both the discomfort from the egg mass and the anxiety associated with egg-laying.

The easiest thing to try for an anxious lizard that appears ready to lay eggs and

Newly hatched babies should be placed in a bin or tank to rest for twenty-four hours before feeding.

can't is to make sure that the egg-laying site is appropriate. Use a deep, large storage tote as a nest box and fill the box three-quarters full with damp horticultural vermiculite pushed up on one side to form a hill. Make sure that it is wet enough to hold together but not so wet that it is like mud. If the mix is too dry, the top could crumble down on her when she digs the hole and turns around to lay. If it is too wet, she may exhaust herself in the effort to dig.

In the event that a female bearded dragon is continuing to have problems, see a veterinarian right away. One of the most common problems is muscle weakness associated with subclinical calcium deficiency. The dragon's calcium isn't low enough for her to show other outward signs but is low enough to interfere with muscle contraction in her oviducts. Some dragons may be weakened by concurrent problems with parasitic, nutritional, viral, or bacterial diseases. This isn't a time to wait and see what happens; doing so is risking the female's life. It is most important to get a diagnosis and try to correct the problem so that she can lay the eggs successfully. In some cases, surgery might be necessary to save the female.

Finally, it is a myth that a single female will not produce eggs. She can. And because the eggs will be infertile, they can be much harder for the female to lay. If you would rather not deal with this risk, and you are looking for a pet bearded dragon rather than a bearded dragon for breeding, you may wish to purchase a male.

RESPIRATORY INFECTIONS

When compared to other groups of lizards, members of the genus *Pogona* tend to be rather resistant to respiratory infections. Nonetheless, prolonged exposure to temperatures that are marginally cool but not quite cold enough to induce brumation can result in respiratory infections in bearded dragons. The most

This dragon displays goiters in the neck and facial deformity from MBD.

obvious symptoms of respiratory infections are gaping, forced exhalation of air, puffing of the throat, and a puffed-up appearance of the body. In severe cases, mucus will accumulate in the mouth and may emerge from the nostrils.

Remember that bearded dragons are desert dwellers. In mild respiratory infections, keep the animals at higher temperatures, with daytime highs in the upper 80s to low 90s Fahrenheit (about 30 to to 33° Celsius), to allow immune system stimulation, enabling the lizard to fight off the infections. If the symptoms persist or worsen, take the animal to a reptile veterinarian for antibiotic therapy. Author Philippe de Vosjoli reports intermittent gaping behavior in heavily parasitized lizards and also in overheated bearded dragons. Respiratory disease is most often associated with subnormal temperatures.

EYE PROBLEMS

Veterinarians across the country have noted that bearded dragons are prone to developing swollen and runny eyes. A common hypothesis for this condition is that dust from sandy substrates is irritating, setting up an inflammatory conjunctivitis that is soon complicated by infections. This is somewhat puzzling, as bearded dragons originate primarily from the red deserts of Australia, where they are certainly exposed to a bit of sand. In any case, unprocessed silica sands and calcium-based sand products can certainly produce profound irritation if a few particles become trapped behind the third eyelid. Most of these problems respond nicely to a temporary change of substrate to newspaper for a couple of weeks while you administer an artificial tears ointment or eye drop two to three times daily. The drops and ointment hydrate the eye and allow small particles to be flushed out.

In resistant cases, an ophthalmic antibiotic drop or ointment may be indicated for an infection. However, some veterinarians report that they still see dragons with eye problems, even with substrate changes and aggressive topical treatment. Other potential causes include allergic, nutritional, traumatic, or viral infections.

Foreign bodies can irritate a bearded dragon's prominent eyes.

YELLOW FUNGUS

Yellow fungus, the *Chrysosporium* anamorph of *Nannizziopsis vriesii* (CANV) begins as yellow or brown crust on the surface of scales and becomes increasingly worse. As the disease progresses, it can internalize, leading to poor appetite, weight loss, and eventually death. Any reptile is susceptible to this disease, which is typically caused by crowded, unsanitary conditions.

Toe injuries and bite marks seem to open the bearded dragon to this fungal infection, and crowded, dirty conditions create stress. Stress suppresses the immune system, so the dragon is unable to fight off the fungus. That said, some dragons do contract this fungal disease even under good husbandry conditions. However, good husbandry and cleanliness will go a long away to prevent yellow fungus infections.

If you suspect that your bearded dragon has yellow fungus, a trip to the vet is required. It is contagious, so all reptiles in the same enclosure should be checked. Oral antifungals have shown the best results, but most infected reptiles will die within eighteen months.

LOSS OF TAIL OR DIGITS

Parts of the tails and digits of juvenile bearded dragons are sometimes nipped off by cagemates. Unlike in many other lizard species, caudal autonomy, or the dropping of part of the tail, is not part of the defensive repertoire of bearded dragons. Once lost, neither tail nor digits will grow back. Fortunately, infections seldom develop following these cannibalistic injuries. However, if the injured dragon is left in with its cannibalistic cagemate, the aggressor may continue to bite and chew at the other dragon's injury, making the situation much worse.

THE HARDY BEARDED DRAGON

Are bearded dragons bulletproof? Obviously, they are not. However, bearded dragons are hardy lizards. This list of ailments should not discourage you from owning and caring for one. Many of these diseases are more problematic in breeding colonies than with just one or two dragons. Bearded dragons are extremely entertaining and gentle, making them one of the best lizards for hands-on activities.

Purchase your dragon from a reputable source. It is a good idea to have your new bearded dragon checked by a qualified vet once it has settled in, it is eating well, and its belly marks (which are a sign

The bearded dragon's long tail can be subject to injury or even cannibalism.

of stress) are gone. At the very least, you need to have your vet perform fecal examinations; if your veterinarian doesn't suggest these tests, then he or she is doing you a disservice.

Eliminate any and all parasites. Quarantine (for parasites and viral diseases) any new bearded dragons. If you own a group of bearded dragons, and one dies, refrigerate it until it can be necropsied by your reptile veterinarian.

In this chapter, the most common diseases of bearded dragons have been discussed. Other diseases occur, too, albeit less frequently. Dragons may require surgery for such problems as broken bones, bite wounds, and placement of drains or feeding tubes. Today's dragons may receive CAT scans and laser surgeries, and they may be examined with ultrasound and endoscopes. If your dragon becomes ill, find a veterinarian who enjoys dragons and is experienced in the medical and surgical care of reptiles.

The following health chart will help you determine whether your dragon needs veterinary care or other treatment for common symptoms.

Troubleshooting Health Chart

Symptoms	Most Common Cause	Treatment
EYES		
Swollen and sore	Foreign bodies; usually related to sandy substrates or calcium sand products	Flush with artificial tears or ointment. Use newspaper substrate until resolved. May need antibiotic ointment for secondary infections.
NOSTRILS		
Occluded (plugged) with open-mouth breathing	Dried secretions from respiratory infections	Apply ointment twice daily until softened. A blunt probe may be required to mechanically remove the plug once softened. Observe for further signs of respiratory disease.
Raw, swollen, or abraded nose	Rostral abrasion	Much less common than in other lizards. Enclosure should be evaluated for size, sharp edges, and availability of hiding spots. Mild abrasions can be treated with Neosporin® or Polysporin®.
MOUTH		
Mild distortion, hemorrhage, viscous secretions, or cheeselike pus. Excess salivation.	Infectious stomatitis (mouth rot)	Unusual in bearded dragons and usually secondary to weakened oral tissues as seen with low calcium. Increase heat; offer a good basking gradient. Gently clean oral tissue with dilute Betadine®, removing all loose and dead tissue. For all but the mildest cases, see veterinarian for antibiotics and to correct underlying conditions.
THROAT		
Distended or inflated; appears to bulge	Usually associated with respiratory infections	Increase heat (thermal gradient). If dragon is in respiratory distress, gently open mouth and attempt to make sure the mouth/throat is clear of debris. See veterinarian for all but mild cases.

Symptoms	Most Common Cause	Treatment
RESPIRATORY SYSTEM (glotttis/trachea)		
Gaping, open-mouth breathing, forced exhalation. Puffed appearance. Frothy and excessive saliva.	Respiratory infection. Intermittent gaping also seen with overheating and threat behavior.	Increase heat (thermal gradient). If in respiratory distress, gently open mouth and attempt to make sure the mouth/throat is clear of debris. See veterinarian for all but the mildest cases to obtain systemic antibiotics, expectorants, drying agents, and nebulization, if needed.
NEUROLOGICAL SYSTEM		
Depressed, decreased appetite, weak, not displaying normal behavior	Signs of a sick bearded dragon but not specific.	See reptile veterinarian to determine whether animal is affected by parasites, viruses, nutritional deficiencies, bacterial agents, etc. At the very least, a fecal examination needs to be performed. Don't miss your chance to get help.
Head tilt, balance off, altered gait, flipping	Inner ear infections. Also seen with head trauma, overheating, bacterial meningitis, toxins and viruses.	Need veterinary exam, as inner ear infections require systemic antibiotics, and central nervous system disorders may require steroid anti-inflammatory drugs. An accurate diagnosis and aggressive supportive care are vital.
Tremors, loss of body functions, spasms	Number of potential causes, including hypocalcemia (low calcium), hypoglycemia (low blood sugar), trauma, bacterial or viral infections, toxins, etc.	Diagnosis is critical to differentiate low blood calcium from low blood sugar. Dragons that have low blood calcium have mild muscle tremors and twitching that is different from seizures originating with the central nervous system. Potentially life-threatening. A common cause is low calcium levels in juvenile animals that respond well to treatment for hypocalcemia.

Symptoms	Most Common Cause	Treatment
SKIN		
Excess dried skin with edges that are peeled up but will not come off	Retained shed	Bearded dragons are used to a dry environment and rarely have trouble. If lightly adhered, hold area underwater and gently rub skin off. If firmly adhered, do not force for fear of tearing skin. Add plastic hiding box with dampened sphagnum moss and wait for skin to loosen. Light misting of cage OK while shedding.
Defined areas of dry, shrunken, adhered scales	Adhered secretions secondary to skin damage by mites and/or bacteria. Also possible burn from basking light.	Look carefully for mites. If found, refer to page 155. An antibacterial cream such as silver sulfadiazine (best), Neosporin, or Polysporin applied twice daily until lesion is resolved works best. Newspaper substrate is best whenever applying creams or ointments. See veterinarian for lesions that aren't resolving.
Abscesses, cysts	Firm granulomas (mass of inflamed granulation tissue, usually associated with infection), rarely tumors	See veterinarian for diagnosis. Needle biopsies are quick and easy. Treatment usually consists of surgical removal or lancing/debridement. Medications are dependent on cause. If abscesses are commonly encountered, move cagemates.
BODY		
Not gaining weight despite eating well. Behavior relatively normal.	Parasitism	Fecal examination is a must. If parasites are diagnosed, refer to the parasite section starting on page 149. It is difficult to eliminate coccidia but worth the effort. Treating the environment is as important as treating the bearded dragons when dealing with parasites with a direct life cycle (i.e., coccidia or pinworms). There is possibility of pinworms, even if proglottids or eggs are not identified.
Puffy, bloated appearance	Gravid (pregnant) females, respiratory infection	Pregnant females tend to appear and feel more plump when nearing egg-laying. Prepare cage for egg-laying. If accompanied by gaping, open-mouth breathing, forced exhalation, excessive salivation, etc., then a respiratory infection should be suspected. Refer to the respiratory section on page 173 for treatment suggestions.

Symptoms	Most Common Cause	Treatment
GASTROINTESTINAL		
Puffy, bloated and painful straining to defecate. Tail swishing. Standing to avoid contact with abdomen.	Constipation, gastrointestinal foreign body	Adding vegetables to the diet may be all that is required to correct the problem. Fecal mass can often be palpated, and warm water enema might be required. Manipulation of colon under sedation might be necessary. Nonresolving cases or those that palpate a firm, cylindrical mass should have X-ray taken for a potential foreign body. Exploratory surgery may be indicated.
Fetid, runny stools	Gastroenteritis, parasites	Fecal examination is a must. Fecal culture may be required if diarrhea doesn't respond to antibiotic treatment.
Weight loss, weakness, poor appetite	Parasites	Fecal examination is a must. If parasites are diagnosed, refer to parasite section starting on page 149.
MUSCULAR/SKELETAL		
Reluctance to move, swollen and painful legs, distorted or kinked tail, soft jaw	Metabolic bone disease (MBD), calcium deficiency	Calcium deficiency may result from either lack of calcium in diet, being fed excessive phosphorus, or a lack of vitamin D_3. Very mild cases will respond to a corrected diet and calcium supplementation. Bearded dragons in pain and reluctant to eat should be seen for calcium injections and vitamin D_3 (if indicated by dietary history). Refer to Chapter 5 for nutrition information.
Fused, distorted vertebrae	Sequelae (pathological conditions that result from disease) to MBD	During episodes of calcium deficiency, bone may be broken down, leading to more brittle and weaker bones, leading to pathological fractures. If calcium becomes available, these previously weak and fractured areas become overmineralized to compensate and form bony lumps.

CHAPTER 11

TRAINING, ENRICHMENT, AND FUN

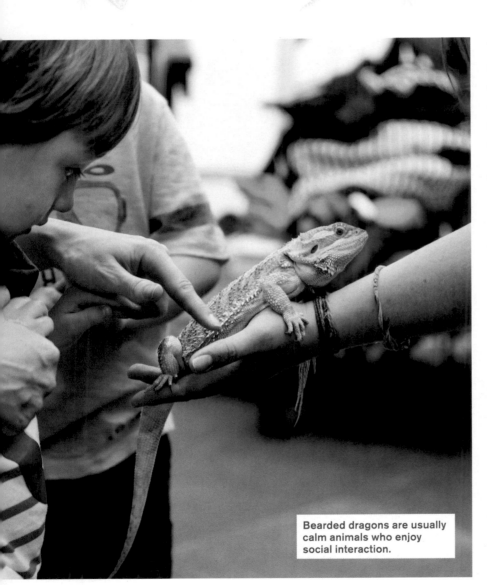

Bearded dragons are usually calm animals who enjoy social interaction.

You may have already noticed that your beardie knows his name, and, if you feed him on a regular schedule, he may wait for his food at mealtime. But have you thought about training your beardie?

You may wonder why you'd want to train your dragon at all. Obviously, you can't train him to sit up and beg—his body type isn't made for that. But what if you'd like him in a certain spot for nail trimming? If he's loose on the floor, would you like him to come when called? Is it easier to pick him up when he's in a specific area of the tank?

Anything you do with your bearded dragon, including these practical behaviors, adds enrichment to his life. He doesn't have to forage for food or worry about predators, so training will give him some mental exercise. Also, the more you do with your beardie, the easier it will be to handle him and the less stressed he will be if he has to visit the veterinarian.

CLICKER TRAINING

The bottom line is that bearded dragons can be trained, and clicker training is the way to do it. If you've trained any other animals and didn't use clicker training, you may have relied on a collar and leash, a halter, or a bridle. You can't use any of those items on your bearded dragons, but you can use a clicker and a target stick to help communicate to your dragon what you want him to do.

To make a target stick, get a small dowel or another straight stick. Tape or glue a colorful lid to one end of your stick. A lid from a peanut butter or mayonnaise jar will work well—you want a lid that is too large for your beardie to bite and offers a nice, large "target" area. (I have seen videos of people using a laser pointer instead of a stick to lure a dragon to perform a behavior, but this is not recommended as there is too much risk of pointing it at your dragon's eyes.)

In addition to your target stick, you'll need a clicker. A clicker is a small plastic device that fits in the palm of your hand and makes a clicking noise when you press it. You can buy a clicker in most pet-supply stores or online. Many books on clicker training also come with a clicker.

The clicker fits in your hand and is simple to use.

Clicker training was originally used to train aquatic mammals, then became popular with dog trainers, and now is used successfully with a wide range of animals. It works the same way with any animal: the "click" sound acts as a marker to tell the animal that what he just did was correct. The clicker also tells the animal that there's a reward coming, and that reward is usually food.

Most worms are too big to use as training rewards. Instead, use tiny bits of a favorite food.

Dragon Agility

Once you and your beardie are working well together with the target stick, you can make a tiny agility course for your dragon with a tunnel to go through, an A-frame to go up and over, and maybe even weave poles. (Weave poles are challenging and require a lot of patience to teach!).

While your beardie may enjoy crickets, roaches, or superworms, these don't work well as training rewards. Most beardies love waxworms, but their high fat content means you have to use them sparingly. Instead, offer tiny bits of food that your dragon can eat quickly and that he doesn't have to chase. If your beardie particularly loves a certain fruit or vegetable, use tiny pieces of that. Offer the treats with a pair of long tweezers or on the tip of a stick. If you train at mealtimes, offer bits of his regular food as the reward, but be aware that it will take your dragon a bit longer to swallow.

The first step in clicker training is to teach your beardie that when he hears the clicker, he's going to get a reward. This requires "charging the clicker." To do this, click the clicker and immediately give your beardie the reward you've chosen. Repeat ten to

A proper harness fits around the dragon's front legs, not around his neck.

twelve times, at which point your beardie should be making the connection that a click means a tasty treat. Because you need so many repetitions to charge the clicker, mealtime might be the best time for this part of the training.

Once you've charged the clicker, you're ready to use your target stick. Slowly introduce the target stick into your dragon's enclosure. If he moves toward it or indicates in any way that he sees it, click and treat. Your goal is to get your dragon to eventually touch the target (the lid on the end of the stick) by rewarding his behavior in increments toward this goal. For instance, if you clicked when he turned his head toward the target, next time wait until he takes a step toward the target to click again.

Once your beardie learns that touching the target means a treat, he will follow the target, so you can use the target stick to move him around the enclosure. Let's say you want your dragon to move to a particular spot. Put down a square of vinyl in a color that contrasts with the floor of his home. Use the target stick to guide him to the spot, then click, treat, and give him attention. Your beardie will soon learn that he gets rewarded when he's on that spot.

If you have a harness and would like to take your dragon outside, or dress him up for Halloween or the family holiday card, using the clicker can help him adjust to a harness. Put the harness in his enclosure and, when he investigates it, click and treat. When he's comfortable with being near the harness, put it on him, click and treat, and take it off. Repeat this over several training sessions, and he'll soon associate the harness with good things. **Note:** Don't leave the harness in the enclosure unless you're training! Left unattended, your beardie might get tangled in the harness and hurt himself.

Your bearded dragon will enjoy spending time with you outside his habitat.

ENRICHMENT ACTIVITIES

If you have no interest in training your beardie, consider other forms of enrichment. A tiny cat toy is something new to discover. An empty cardboard tube can be fun to explore. (Just make sure the tube is large enough so your lizard won't get stuck inside.) Your dragon might enjoy pushing a small ball around his home. Give him a dandelion, a marigold, or a petunia to check out—he can smell, touch, and even eat these flowers.

On the same subject, scents can be a source of enrichment. Crush fresh herbs or put a tiny pinch of dried herbs in the enclosure. While herbs shouldn't be part of your beardie's everyday diet, you can add them occasionally to his food. Offering a small amount will encourage him to hunt for where the smell is located. Basil, dill, catnip, oregano, lemon balm, thyme, rosemary, chives, sage, and peppermint are all safe herbs for your beardie.

People with dogs can participate in "nosework," in which the dogs are trained to locate specific scents in specific areas, such as a room or car or outdoor area. There's no such organized sport for bearded dragons—in fact, in the case of the beardie, it should be called "tongue work" because that tiny forked tongue allows the beardie to both smell and taste his environment—but you can have fun trying something similar anyway! (See Tongue-Tasting on page 117.) Get your clicker and those tasty treats, and when your dragon explores a specific scent, click and treat. Eventually, you can have tiny piles of three or four herbs, and he will pick out the one you have trained him to choose. If you decide to try this activity with your beardie, don't let him eat those training herbs every day. They're fine now and then but shouldn't be fed regularly.

An easy and fun way to give your dragon enrichment is to take him out of his enclosure indoors. If you have a young dragon, limit his time out to a few minutes at a time and no more than forty minutes total per day. Your adult beardie can have up to two hours of total time out of his enclosure per day, but pay close attention to the temperature, and don't take him out right after a meal. Beardies need time in the controlled warmth of their enclosure to properly digest their food.

Many beardies enjoy snuggling up to something soft.

If you're going to let your dragon roam free, be sure to watch him at all times. This is not the time to text your friend. Pay attention to your dragon only. Keep any other pets in the household away from your bearded dragon, in another area of the house. There may be instances of friendship between a dog or cat and a beardie, but it's more likely that your dog or cat will frighten your dragon or, in the worst case, injure him or try to eat him.

Some bearded dragons love to look out the window. Some seem very content to snuggle up and watch television with you. Others enjoy time outdoors, and some owners like to take their beardies out in enclosed pet strollers to ensure their safety. Sometimes your dragon will simply want to be held or to rest on your shoulder. Bearded dragons truly bond with their people, and time with you daily may be all the enrichment your dragon needs.

JUST FOR FUN

A lot goes into setting up the perfect bearded dragon habitat, but once you've done that, it's time for the fun stuff. You can decorate the enclosure with a scenic backdrop, you can provide basking spots and hideaways of interesting sizes and shapes, and you can even add a small sofa or a small chaise lounge. While this may sound a bit silly, beardies do enjoy cuddling up on soft materials, and you might find that dragon-sized furniture is one of his favorite things. Furniture comes in a variety of fabric color and styles, so your dragon's décor can match your own.

A harness is a necessary accessory if you plan to take your dragon outdoors. Beardies are fast, and you don't want to lose yours and have him fall prey to a dog or cat. Harnesses are available through various online pet-supply shops. Make sure that the harness you buy goes around your beardie's front legs, not around his neck. Also remember that the harness is just a way to keep your beardie safe outdoors. You can't expect to "walk" your dragon like a dog, and you cannot yank or pull him around; a bearded dragon's bones are fragile. If you want to move your dragon, pick him up.

If you want to dress up your dragon, you can find harnesses with wings attached: think angel wings for Christmas or bat or dragon wings for Halloween. If Halloween is one of your favorite holidays, your beardie can join the celebration with his own costume. Do a quick online search for "bearded dragon Halloween costumes," and you'll see dragons dressed as sharks, pirates, pumpkins, and more. You can even find hats, hoodies, and sweaters in many different types and styles for your beardie.

Make sure that anything your beardie wears fits properly. Too loose, and your dragon could get tangled; too tight, and circulation to his legs or tail might be restricted. Also, don't leave any costume or clothing on for too long. As cute as it might be, and as calm as your dragon might be when you dress

Shallow water and supervision are needed for your beardie to take a swim.

him, your dragon doesn't really need clothes. Of course, he doesn't need a skateboard and helmet, either, but he can have one of each!

Not all bearded dragons like swimming, but swimming in a shallow pan or bowl can be good exercise for your beardie if he enjoys it. A few words of caution about swimming: Do not allow your bearded dragon to swim in a pool. The high chlorine levels in pool water can dry out your dragon's skin and can harm him if he drinks it. Most tap water is fine. Also, the chances of your dragon drowning in a pool are much greater than in an inch or two of water. Be sure to supervise your dragon's swimming time. A beardie who likes the water might also enjoy relaxing on a dragon-sized float, such as a rubber duck, flamingo, or watermelon—yes, you can find these on Amazon!

Your beardie is not the only one who can have fun accessories. There are many novelty items for beardie owners, too. Show your love for your bearded dragon with a pin, earrings, or a necklace. Etsy and Amazon are good places to start. Café Press has wonderful sweatshirts and T-shirts with slogans like, "Just a girl who loves beardies," and "I have a reptile dysfunction." Or get a plaque for your wall that reads, "Life is good, but bearded dragons make it better," or "Warning: This property is protected by a highly trained bearded dragon." Drink your morning tea or coffee from a mug adorned with a bearded dragon. There are even sheets and bedspreads printed with lifelike images of bearded dragons.

CHAPTER 12

FREQUENTLY ASKED QUESTIONS

Q New Juvenile Will Not Eat

I just brought home my juvenile bearded dragon, and he will not eat. What is the problem?

A This is the most frequently asked question from new owners, but the answer could be one of several reasons. Let's assume the problem is not illness related.

- First, assess your setup. What size tank are you using? It needs to be a 20-gallon (76L) long tank, which measures 30 inches long by 12 inches tall (76 x 31cm).
- Second, what are the temperatures on top of the basking rock and on the cool side floor? They should be 95 to 100°F (35 to 38°C) and 80°F (27°C), respectively.
- Next, look at your setup—is it as simple as possible? There should be a basking rock, a water bowl, and a flat salad plate—and that is all. Crickets and other insects can hide if the tank has too many items in it. Babies need to be able to find food items easily and are sometimes frightened by a tank full of climbing structures, plants, or hammocks. Keep it simple.
- Then, examine your approach to water. A dehydrated dragon will not eat. Is he being misted in the early morning with hot tap water and in the late evening with warm tap water?
- Finally, placing white printer paper around all four sides of the tank can calm him down until he gets used to his new environment.

Q Juvenile Dragon Not Eating Greens

I give my dragon greens every day on the cool side of the tank, but he never eats them. How can I get my juvenile bearded dragon to eat his greens?

A Generally, bearded dragons prefer not to go to the cool side to eat greens. Place greens

on the hot side, almost right in front of the dragons while they bask. Tear the greens, like you would if making a salad, rather than chopping them fine. Do not mist greens because this can cause bacteria to flourish. If the greens dry out under the heat and become crisp, that is perfectly fine. Some dragons prefer them that way!

Q Parasites in Adult Bearded Dragons

I have an adult bearded dragon that will not eat. Could the problem be parasites?

A

There are many parasites that plague reptiles, and a few are deadly to bearded dragons, especially in captive environments. The most common parasites, coccidia, pinworms, and amebiasis, are acquired through contaminated prey items, food, water, and cages. The most important thing you can do is to be on the alert for signs of parasites in dragons. These signs include:

- Refusal to feed.
- Weight loss. Invest in a gram scale. Weigh your adult dragon every week as a tool for assessing his health.
- Diarrhea, mucus or blood in stools, or a change in color or smell of stools.
- Inactivity. Healthy dragons are alert, bright-eyed, and usually standing erect.
- Dehydrated appearance. Dehydrated dragons have a sunken look to the eyes and dark semicircles under the back halves of the lower lids.

There are hundreds of parasites that can attack lizards, but three stand out as the most commonly seen in bearded dragons: coccidia, pinworms, and amebiasis, the latter caused by entamoeba.

Coccidia: Common protozoan that generally does not cause the animal any problems in the wild but can wreak havoc in captivity. Symptoms include mild to severe diarrhea, anorexia (refusal to feed), weakness,

lethargy, and death. Diagnosis is made by fecal smear or flotation on fresh stool. Treatment: Ponazuril.

Pinworms: Very common in lizards, pinworms live in the lower GI tract. Diagnosis is by fecal flotation. Treatment: Panacur.

Amebiasis: This protozoan can be extremely lethal. Some animals carry it with no problem while others waste and die. According to Dr. Klingenberg, clinical signs are highly variable but include anorexia, dehydration, and mucus-laden or bloody stools. Diagnosis can require analysis of several fresh smears to identify amoebas, or multi-nucleated cysts, in the stool. Treatment: Metronidazole.

What you can do:
- Take your dragon and a fresh stool sample to a reptile vet to be checked for parasites.
- Use paper towels as a substrate. This helps break the cycle of recontamination.

- Clean water and food dishes daily, disinfecting with a diluted bleach-and-water solution.
- Do not recycle prey food from the cage back to the cricket bin or from one cage to another.
- Do not leave uneaten crickets in cages.
- Wash your hands after handling reptiles.
- If you use sand as substrate and support a colony of dragons, never use the same sand scoop for multiple cages.

Q **Bearded Dragons and Dogs and Cats**
We want to get a juvenile bearded dragon, but we have a cat. Is this a problem?

A Juvenile bearded dragons are low on the food chain in Australia, so it is realistic to expect the dragon to be frightened of a cat or a dog at this stage of his life. Keep in mind that there are feral cats in Australia that prey on baby bearded dragons. A baby

bearded dragon seems to be more afraid of cats than of dogs at this age in terms of what he can see from his tank. In either case, it's recommended to keep the dragon in a separate room for a few months as he grows up. If this is not possible, use a screen lid with appropriate cutouts for the basking bulb and UVB tube (screens block some UVB and create a darker environment). Once the baby dragon has grown into an adult, he is more likely to become friends with the cat or dog. It depends a lot on the disposition of the cat/dog. The bottom line? Keep the baby lizard separated and safe until he is larger, higher on the food chain, less fragile, and more relaxed and then carefully introduce them to each other in a protected and safe environment. This is not to say that some cats/dogs would not attack the dragon in any stage of his life. Only you know your situation. Use caution and common sense.

Q How Many to Feed?
How many bugs should my juvenile bearded dragon eat each day?

A Juvenile bearded dragons eat a lot! So the answer is that your bearded dragon should be allowed to eat as many insects as he will eat in a 30-minute period, twice a day. Some juveniles will eat 30 or even more than 50 per day, depending on the size of the juvenile and the type of feeder insect. Do not dump a lot of crickets in the baby's enclosure all at once; instead, throw in up to five at a time and see if the dragon starts eating right away. If it does, add a few more; if it doesn't, walk away, come back 30 minutes later, and remove uneaten feeder insects (except black soldier fly larvae, which can stay in the tank all day).

Q What Sex?

How can I tell the sex of my juvenile bearded dragon?

A

If you are new to bearded dragons and have a juvenile, the safest way is to first check for a wide base of the head. A wide skull usually indicates a male. You can also check for prominent femoral pores on the inside thighs, which would also indicate a male. The width of the base of the tail can also be used to determine sex in babies. Males have a wider tail base. Females have a narrower tail base.

For experienced bearded dragon handlers, there's another option. Hold the dragon face out, straight along the palm of your hand. Very gently, raise the tail toward the ceiling and then check the area right above the vent. If the dragon is male, there will be two vertical bulges (the hemipenes) on either side of a tunnel. The area will be flat or have one bump if the dragon is female. It is difficult to

be 100-percent accurate at sexing a 6-inch (15cm) bearded dragon. This method can be very dangerous if the person attempting to sex the dragon is inexperienced. It is possible to cause permanent or lethal back and other injuries to the dragon.

With large subadult and adult bearded dragons, it becomes easier to tell the sex by observation. For example, by five or six months of age, males are typically displaying a black beard and head-bobbing behavior.

Q Color Morph Bearded Dragon Looks Gray

My juvenile bearded dragon was brightly colored when I opened the shipping box from the breeder, but now he is gray. What is going on?

A

Although there seem to be differing opinions on what setup is best for juvenile bearded dragons, one thing is certain: if the dragon is

bright in color and shows a pure white belly with no striations or dark pattern and eats voraciously, the dragon is happy. Stressed dragons are dark in color. And as sure as stress will sicken humans, it will sicken bearded dragons, too. If the dragon shows signs of stress, rethink your setup. Are the basking and cool side temperatures correct? Is the tank full of items that are stressing him out? Can he see too much activity in the room? TV? Phones? Video games? Identify the problem(s). You will know that you've solved the problem when the dragon becomes bright again.

Q Size Tank for Juvenile Bearded Dragon

My breeder recommended a 20-gallon (76L) long tank for a few months for my juvenile bearded dragon and then a forever tank of 55-gallons (208L). Can I just go to the 55-gallon (208L) tank and save the money?

A This would be unwise. Juvenile bearded dragons need a smaller tank so that they're more easily able to hunt for insects. Crickets will run to the cool side of the tank to get away from the light, but if the dragon is sitting under the basking light in a too-big tank, he will not find the crickets. Additionally, UVB does not penetrate at the therapeutic level beyond a certain length. The 20-gallon (76L) long tank is 12 inches (31cm) high, which is the perfect size for a juvenile to to thrive.

Q Bearded Dragons' Defecation Habits

My bearded dragon has not gone to the bathroom in two weeks. Is this normal?

A Bearded dragons should eat and defecate every single day. The problem with your dragon could be any of a number of things: husbandry or temperature issues, improper foods, a parasite, or even a blocked

intestine from ingesting sand. Do not wait any longer—please take him to a qualified veterinarian right away.

Q Bearded Dragon Feces as Health Indicators

My bearded dragon's stools look like dark matter and some white stuff. Is this normal?

A

Yes. Healthy bearded dragons produce dark, formed to semi-formed feces with white urates.

Q Superworm Myth

I've heard that superworms can eat through the stomachs of bearded dragons. Is this true?

A

False. While superworms have powerful jaws, a superworm has never actually eaten through a bearded dragon's stomach. The bearded dragon's stomach acid starts to dissolve prey items immediately. That said, make sure

that the temperatures in the enclosure are correct for bearded dragon digestion and you are not feeding superworms late at night and then turning off the lights. Also, feed superworms to large subadults and adults only. Remove any superworms in the cage after thirty minutes. Superworms can bite a bearded dragon's face, lips, and toes.

Q Lights On and Off

How many hours a day should lights stay on?

A

Light schedules can change depending on the season. For example, in the northeastern United States, indoor dragons can get 12 hours of UVB and basking light and 12 hours with all lights off each day. Then, in the peak of summer, switch to 14 hours on and 10 hours off; in winter, 10 hours on and 14 hours off unless the dragon is brumating.

Q Bearded Dragons and Water Bowls
Do bearded dragons drink from a bowl?

A
If you are talking about a bearded dragon in an indoor enclosure, the answer is rarely. Because bearded dragons bask at higher temperatures all day, it is important to mist babies twice a day and mist adult dragons once a day plus give them one daily soak. The purpose of a water dish is primarily so that the dragon can lie down, stretch out to full length, and soak. Therefore, you want the water dish to be as long as the dragon's body and about shoulder high. New owners sometimes create a juvenile setup with a small, deep, corner-type water dish, which is not good for a bearded dragon.

It's important to note that nighttime soaks need to be two hours after the dragon's dinner because soaking cools him down and stops digestion.

Q Death in Small Tanks
I bought a bearded dragon three months ago and set him up in the 10-gallon (38L) tank that the pet store sold me along with a spotlight and hot rock. He did well until recently, when he started gaping and stopped feeding. He died two days ago. What happened?

A
This is a common scenario when baby bearded dragons are raised in tanks that are too small. Initially, because they are small, they can move away from the heat sources, but as they grow larger, their increased body size makes it impossible to escape the heat. Bearded dragons don't just grow in length, they also grow in height and width, exposing them to more heat the larger they are.

The typical sequence of events is that the dragon first starts panting in a desperate attempt to cool off. He then stops eating because survival is becoming his primary concern. Finally, he overheats and dies. Because of their rapid growth rate, bearded dragons cannot be reared past three or four weeks of age in a 10-gallon (38L) tank. Next time, start with a 20-gallon (76L) long tank for a juvenile dragon.

Q Death in Small Tanks: Another Scenario
I recently bought a baby bearded dragon along with a 10-gallon (38L) tank and a 100-watt mercury vapor bulb. The baby died. What happened?

A This is another common scenario with baby bearded dragons. In a 10-gallon (38L) tank, a 100-watt bulb can generate so much heat that it will literally cook the baby. Even if the dragon can initially get away from the heat,

it won't be long before he grows larger and gets stuck in the hot zone. Bulbs of 60–75 watts are adequate for smaller tanks, but a 10-gallon (38L) tank is not the proper size for rearing a baby bearded dragon. Remember: a 20-gallon (76L) long tank is the correct size, and bearded dragons need a sizeable cool area to escape excessive heat.

Q Thermometers: Not All Are Equal
I just lost my baby bearded dragon, and I don't know why. All of the temperatures were correct according to the strip thermometer on the tank wall that came with my tank.

A Not all thermometers are created equal. The strip-type thermometers are good for fish in a tank but not for bearded dragons. There are many types of reptile thermometers, from simple round thermometers to digital probes and infrared digital temperature guns, which will give you a more accurate reading. With

temperatures being so critical to the health of a bearded dragon, it cannot be a guessing game—you need a good thermometer.

Q Darkness and Feeding

I have a couple of half-grown bearded dragons in a 4-foot (1.2m) tank with a 75-watt spotlight for heat at one end. The problem is that they don't seem interested in eating, and they sleep all the time. Should I take them to a veterinarian?

A

Don't rush to the vet just yet. This is another common problem with bearded dragons that are not set up correctly. It happens in pet stores all the time. Bearded dragons are diurnal animals that derive psychological benefits from a high level of light. A single spotlight on a large tank means that most of the tank will be too dark. A consequence of low light is poor appetite. You should have full-spectrum, high-UVB, fluorescent reptile

bulbs running the length of your tank and turned on for up to 14 hours a day. If, after a couple of weeks, your dragons don't perk up and show significant improvement in appetite and activity, then you should take them to a qualified reptile veterinarian. Beware, however, of veterinarians inexperienced with bearded dragons. They can sometimes do more harm than good.

Of course, the inexpensive alternative to UVB bulbs is to allow bearded dragons regular exposure to sunlight for many hours during the warm months, providing you have a climate conducive to a reptile and a location to protect your dragon from poisonous snakes, fire ants, and lightning bugs (fireflies).

Q Is UVB Really Necessary?

Is it possible to raise bearded dragons without using a source of UV light, such as the special reptile UVB bulbs?

A Some owners have raised the popular species of bearded dragon to adulthood without exposure to UVB, using regular supplementation with vitamin/mineral mixes that contained calcium and vitamin D_3. However, raising these lizards without a UV source is a gamble. With the current method of dusting food with powdered vitamin/mineral supplements, not enough is known about the long-term effectiveness of the formulas and proper dosage.

By far, the most common health complaint with baby bearded dragons continues to be signs of calcium deficiency, such as hind-leg twitching. Exposure to a UV source appears to be the most reliable way to provide these lizards with adequate levels of vitamin D_3 to allow better absorption of calcium. There are other potential benefits, including psychological benefits, of exposure to more balanced lighting that comes closer to natural sunlight. If you live in a sunny area, exposing your lizards to a UV source should be easy and economical during the warmer months of the year. Two to four hours of sunlight a week is probably enough to meet the needs of bearded dragons.

Q **Brumation and False Signs of Disease**
My bearded dragon had been doing well until last month (November) when he started spending most of his time hidden. He has also refused any food, and I'm worried he may be sick.

A Your bearded dragon may not actually be sick. Very likely, you are dealing with brumation and the false signs of disease. Indeed, a common reason first-time dragon owners consult veterinarians is brumation. This is a natural rest period for bearded dragons older than one year of age, and it appears similar to certain signs of disease. During brumation, bearded dragons don't

feed, are inactive, and hide most of the time. An inexperienced veterinarian might recommend unnecessary, costly, and sometimes harmful procedures.

To assess the health of your bearded dragon at this time, consider the following: If this shutdown occurs in the winter, if your dragon is not losing much weight and is maintaining rounded body contours, and if he appears relatively alert and wide-eyed when you pick him up, then he is probably fine and just doing what bearded dragons naturally do at that time of the year. It's most important for you to keep him at cooler temperatures (66 to 70°F [19 to 21°C]) during this period of time. Only in the case of clear signs of disease, such as rapid weight loss, sunken eyes, gaping, forced exhalation, eyes that don't fully open, and a limp rag-doll feel should you bring your dragon to the veterinarian during apparent brumation.

Q Red Lights/Nighttime Heat
Should I use a red light at night?

A Bearded dragons need a nighttime drop in temperature to cool off from the day. Aim for 68 to 70°F (20 to 21°C). If the room falls below this range, a ceramic heat emitter with a dimmer switch is the best option. Make sure that the temperature does not go higher than 70°F (21°C) or lower than 65°F (18°C).

Q Toe-Twitching
I set up my baby bearded dragons just right. They are in a room kept at about 80°F (27°C) with a UVB bulb. They are fed twice daily with ¼-inch (6mm) crickets dusted with calcium and a general vitamin/mineral supplement. This week, a few started twitching, and my vet diagnosed them with calcium deficiency. Where did I go wrong?

A Dietary problems can arise as much from errors in husbandry as from diet, so whenever you're faced with a nutritional problem, take a look at husbandry, too. The problem may not be with diet or supplementation but with light and heat. Dragons respond to a bright light and a basking spot that is warmer than the overall enclosure. Without stimulation from light, baby dragons will likely eat a less-than-optimal number of crickets and develop signs of calcium deficiency. Moreover, such signs don't always have to be due to calcium. Deficiencies of magnesium and glucose can produce similar signs.

For your case specifically, drop the room temperature to about 70 to 75°F (21 to 24°C) and add a bright light that creates a basking spot of about 95 to 100°F (35 to 38°C). Make sure you retain a temperature gradient so that the dragons can select cooler temperatures, too.

Q **Help—My Dragon's Having Convulsions!**
I bought a pair of baby bearded dragons a month ago. They've been eating great and growing rapidly. Suddenly, today I found one having convulsions, and the other one's toes and feet are twitching. What should I do?

A This scenario sounds like a classic case of calcium deficiency in baby dragons. The babies that eat the most and are growing the fastest need the most calcium in order to support such rapid growth. Signs of calcium deficiency include tremors, twitching, seizures, and bloating. Give your dragons calcium immediately; a liquid calcium supplement is a good first step for babies that are twitching or having seizures. Feed only black soldier fly larvae for a few weeks until symptoms subside. Consult a reptile veterinarian for dosage and administration.

Next, evaluate husbandry and diet. Are your dragons exposed to ample UVB from special bulbs? Keep in mind that UVB bulbs do deteriorate, often within six months. If you do not have a UVB meter to measure your bulbs' output, get one—it is a wise purchase. Do your dragons have a source of dietary calcium and dietary vitamin D₃? You may need the help of a qualified veterinarian to correct the immediate problem of hypocalcemia and for advice on fixing the dragons' husbandry and diet.

Q Breeding Age for Females

When can I breed my female? I have read conflicting information.

A

This is probably because all females do not mature at the same rate. Just as female dogs do not come into season at the same

exact age, female bearded dragons ovulate at different ages. A safe rule of thumb in an indoor environment is that the female should weigh at least 350 grams and be at least 12 months of age. At that point, test the female. If she responds to the male by slowly lowering her head and waving her arm, chances are good that she will accept him. If not, try again in a few weeks, and so on.

Q Feeding Spinach and Kale

My friend told me that spinach and kale are bad for dragons, but mine loves these foods. Can I still feed these greens?

A

All greens contain substances generally referred to as secondary plant compounds. Some are helpful to animals, and others can be harmful. Two substances most frequently mentioned as harmful are

oxalates and goitrogens, but there are many other compounds, some even riskier than these two. However, if you avoided every green, fruit, and vegetable that contains a potentially harmful secondary plant compound, there would be nothing left to feed! You can continue to feed spinach and kale to your dragon. Make sure they make up just a moderate part of the overall diet and that you include supplements containing calcium and trace minerals. Don't feed diets of just spinach and kale with no additional supplementation.

Q Mystery Deaths

I thought I was doing what was best for my dragons, but now two are dead! They've been outside for the summer in a screen cage set up with ample shade and areas to bask in the sun. I feed and water them before work each morning and hose out the cage each evening. Last night, about an hour after cage cleaning, I found two of them dead! I know they were feeling OK because they still had bugs in their mouths. What happened?

A While a long-distance diagnosis is impossible, it could be that your dragons died from eating fireflies. These insects, also known as lightning bugs, are especially prevalent in the eastern United States, are active in the evening, and seem to be attracted to damp grass and foliage. In one instance, a breeder lost dozens of adult dragons one summer during a drought when he began hosing the cages in the evening. Fireflies entered the cages and were gobbled up by the dragons. It only takes one firefly to kill a dragon, and death occurs very soon after swallowing the bug. Change your routine so that you're hosing the cages in the morning, prior to feeding, and offering another meal in late afternoon (with no additional hosing) to offset late-day dragon hunger.

Keeping Feeder Crickets Alive

Q How do you keep crickets alive? Mine are always dying right away, and they stink!

A Crickets kept in overcrowded conditions, in a cold area, or in a container with a solid lid will die. The humidity can build up, causing death and odor. To keep 1,000 crickets alive, use a 20-gallon (76L) long tank or 66-quart (62L) clear bin. When crickets arrive, cut open the box, turn it upside down and shake the egg crate and crickets into the bin. The crickets will run from light (the reason for a clear bin) and stay between the egg-crate layers. Then, feed a commercial cricket food and offer water or half of a potato for moisture. Replace uneaten food daily.

"Taming" Bearded Dragons

Q I read online that I need to tame my new juvenile bearded dragon by holding and petting him all the time. Is this true?

A No. If your juvenile is at least 8 inches (20cm) long, handling him gently once a day is fine until he is larger. But most bearded dragons have delightful dispositions and do not need to be "tamed." In fact, constantly harassing a baby by grabbing him in his tank before he is fully acclimated can actually make him distrustful of his new owners. Keep in mind that bearded dragons need to know that you are not a predator but the new "food person."

Sunlight

Q I heard that putting my dragon out in sunlight is best. Is that true?

A It depends on where you are located, what time of year it is, and the outdoor temperature. If it is a spring day on the East Coast, chances are your dragon will be cold, which can cause illness. If you consider your dragon's preferred basking temperature, and if

the outdoor temperature is much lower, don't risk it. If a dragon basks at 100°F (38°C), and it is 60°F (16°C) outside, can you see the problem? Also, when you take your dragon out, be mindful of when he has eaten last. You would not want to feed your dragon and then take him away from basking to go out in a much cooler environment. Bearded dragons need about two hours of heat and light to digest food, so playtime should come after this period of time has passed.

Q Vet Checks
How often should I take my dragon to the vet?

A
If your dragon is asymptomatic, a yearly checkup with fecal flotation to test for coccidia and intestinal worms should be adequate. However, if your dragon is showing symptoms of illness, such as runny stools,

an unpleasant odor, lack of appetite, or listlessness, get him to the vet right away.

Q Bearded Dragons and Skin Shedding
I've had an adult bearded dragon for more than a year and have yet to see him shed his skin. Do bearded dragons shed?

A
Like other reptiles, bearded dragons regularly shed their skin in a single sheet, much like people do after a sunburn. Most reptiles tend to shed frequently when young and less often as they get older. Injury or disease to the skin also results in an increased shedding rate to repair the damage. One way to recognize when a bearded dragon is about to shed is that his coloration appears duller, as if he is covered with a clear white film. This is a sign of the old skin layer being pushed to the surface and separated from the underlying replacement skin.

Bearded dragons shed in broken skin patches that they apparently eat. Various breeders report that they have seldom seen bearded dragons actually shedding or found shed skins in their enclosures, so the dragons very likely consume the skin quickly after shedding. In fact, it is not uncommon to see baby bearded dragons that are kept in a group to pick the shedding skin off of each other. The same may happen with adults.

Q Trouble Shedding

I have a sick baby bearded dragon that is having trouble shedding. Is this common in bearded dragons?

A In bearded dragons, various factors, including disease, diet, and husbandry conditions, can sometimes cause shedding problems. Sick reptiles may be too weak to perform the movements required to remove shed

skin, so it is not unusual to see sick dragons with adhering shed skin. Injuries to the skin that result in scabs or scars can also cause localized adhesion of old skin.

Natural substrates may play a role in helping free shed skin from digits. Diet, including water and vitamin/mineral content of food, can facilitate and even speed up shedding. Providing a varied diet that includes fresh greens and vegetables will help prevent shedding problems.

To remove adhering skin from a sick dragon, keep him on paper substrate and gently mist him with lukewarm water to help soften the adhering skin. Try gently peeling loose skin, using your fingertips or tweezers. It is important that you attempt to remove only loose, white skin that is clearly in the process of coming off. Removing skin during the milky stage when new skin is still forming can cause serious skin injuries.

You can also place a section of cardboard egg carton into the enclosure, place the dragon on top of the cardboard, and mist the dragon until the cardboard is moistened. The dragon will rub himself along the cardboard, which helps remove the shed skin.

Q Visual Perspectives and Breeding

I have a pair of inland bearded dragons that I purchased two years ago, and I have yet to see signs of breeding. They are in a 36-inch (91cm)–long enclosure with a small one-tube fluorescent fixture and an incandescent bulb. What am I doing wrong?

A

It is suprising to hear of people having trouble with breeding their bearded dragons, considering these lizards are among the easiest reptiles to breed. It's likely that the breeding failures are attributed to improper husbandry.

Remember that bearded dragons are diurnal and depend on visual clues to elicit breeding behaviors; thus, a common cause of breeding failure is too small of an enclosure. Bearded dragons benefit from the greater range of visual perspectives and social behaviors possible in larger enclosures. Indoors, an enclosure that measures 48 inches long by 24 inches deep (wide) by 18 or 24 inches high (122 x 61 x 46 or 61cm) is sufficient. Another cause may be inadequate lighting. Animals kept in setups with low levels of light may also fail to breed. A simple method for getting bearded dragons to breed was discovered by a well-known bearded dragon expert. Remove the dragons from their cage and place them on the floor of a room in an area lit by a spotlight. Within minutes, the male will usually head-bob and attempt to breed the female. If she is receptive, you will usually end up with a clutch of fertile eggs.

Q Temperature-Dependent Sex Determination in Bearded Dragons

Based on the sex ratios of bearded dragons hatched in my collection, it appears that incubation temperature could play a role in determining the sex of bearded dragons. Do you think it's possible?

A

Temperature-dependent sex determination (TDSD) is a complex subject best resolved by genetic research and experimentation. The only possible answer at this time is that there are indications that there may be TDSD in bearded dragons. Clutches that were incubated at 82 to 84°F (28 to 29°C) have yielded a higher proportion of males than other clutches that were incubated at 84 to 86°F (29 to 30°C). One breeder reported that a clutch he incubated at 82°F (28°C) yielded mostly males.

TDSD in bearded dragons has yet to be fully understood but will likely be clarified by additional data from breeders who keep careful records of incubation temperatures and monitor hatchlings until their sex can be definitely determined.

Q Removing Bearded Dragons from Eggs that Fail to Hatch

I recently had a clutch of bearded dragon eggs. After the initial collapse that precedes hatching, a number of babies hatched, but several failed to slit the eggs. Could I have manually removed the babies?

A

Manually removing babies from eggs results mostly in failure. At best, you can slit the eggs after twenty-four hours of the initial collapse—and hope. To slit an unhatched egg, use cuticle scissors to penetrate the shell and cut close to the shell, making sure that you do not penetrate past the shell surface. The slit should run through the center third of

the egg. Once the egg is slit, leave it alone. In time, a baby lizard may emerge on its own. Never manually pull a lizard out of the egg following incision.

In spite of these procedures, most lizards that fail to slit their eggs on their own also fail to emerge from manually slit eggs. Of the few that do, most go on to die. In other words, the value of slitting unhatched eggs is questionable.

Q Tail Rot

I now have had several bearded dragons whose tail tips have darkened. This eventually spread and part of the tail was lost. What causes this?

A

The popular term for this kind of tail loss is "tail rot." It is usually attributed to two causes: 1) trauma, such as an injury from being nipped or from being crushed or compressed by landscape materials, and 2) accumulating tail-tip sheds. The first step is to dip the damaged tail in a hydrogen-peroxide solution as soon as you notice the darkened tail. The solution softens the adhering shed skin, allows for its removal, and helps stop infection early on. Dipping the tail in Betadine also works against infection and prevents the spread of tail rot. If neither of these work, consider seeing a qualified reptile veterinarian.

The best weapon against tail rot is prevention: keep babies segregated and well fed, make sure there are no landscape structures that can cause trauma to the tail, and soak bearded dragons in shallow water dishes to soften adhering shed skin.

Q Eyes Bulging

My juvenile dragon's eyes suddenly bulged out. Is this normal?

A

Yes. Bearded dragons will bulge their eyes briefly, although no one is sure why. The most likely reason is to help shed the skin around and on their eyes.

RESOURCES

Bartholomew, G. A., and V. A. Tucker. 1963. Control of Changes in Body Temperature, Metabolism, and Circulation by the Agamid Lizard, *Amphibolurus barbatus*. *Physiological Zoology* 36:199–218.

Bedford, G. S., K. A. Christian, and A. D. Griffiths. 1993. Preliminary Investigations on the Reproduction of the Frillneck Lizard (*Chlamydosarus kingii*) in the Northern Territory. In Lunney, D., and D. Ayers. *Herpetology in Australia*. Transactions of the Royal Zoological Society of New South Wales, 414 s. c. kingii.

De Vosjoli, P., S. Donoghue, and R. Klingenberg. 1999. The Multifactorial Model of Herpetoculture. Part 1: Ontogeny. *The Vivarium*. 11:1.

Hauschild, A. and H. Bosch. 2000. *Bearded Dragons and Frilled Lizards*. Matthias Schmidt Publications. Germany. Highly recommended for anyone interested in these species; has an extensive bibliography.

Klingenberg, R. 1993. *Understanding Reptile Parasites*. Irvine, Calif.: Advanced Vivarium Systems.

Klingenberg, R. 1997. Pinworms: Friend or Foe. *The Vivarium*. 8:5, 23–24.

MacMillen, R. E., M. L. Augee, and B. A. Ellis. 1989. Thermal Ecology and Diet of Some Xerophilous Lizards from Western South Wales. *Journal of Arid Environments* 16:193–201. This is the often-quoted reference on the predominantly plant diet of adult bearded dragons. Also contains valuable information on thermoregulation.

Rossi, J. and R. Rossi. 1996. *What's Wrong with My Snake?* Irvine, Calif.: Advanced Vivarium Systems. 61–64.

Slavens, F. and K. Slavens. 1996, 2000. *Reptiles and Amphibians in Captivity*. Seattle, Wash.: Slaveware.

Weis, P. 1996. Husbandry and Breeding of the Frilled Lizard in *Advances in Herpetoculture*. International Herpetological Symposium.1:87–92.

INDEX

Photographs are denoted by **bold** page numbers.

PHOTO CREDITS

ABOUT THE AUTHORS

Philippe de Vosjoli is an expert on reptile husbandry who revolutionized herpetoculture with the publication of *The Vivarium* magazine and the *Advanced Vivarium Systems* line of books. With over a million books in print, he is the best-selling author of more than 20 books and 100 articles on the care and breeding of amphibians and reptiles. With Robert Mailloux, he pioneered the commercial breeding of bearded dragons and coauthored the best-selling *General Care and Maintenance of Bearded Dragons.*

Robert Mailloux is the owner of Sandfire Dragon Ranch and was responsible for developing the commercial breeding of bearded dragons in the United States. He was the originator of the Sandfire morph of bearded dragon. He is an amphibian specialist and was the first person to commercially breed several of the frog species now readily available in the pet trade. With Philippe de Vosjoli, he has coauthored several articles and books on the herpetoculture of bearded dragons and tropical frogs.

Susan Donoghue, VMD, DACVN, has combined a lifelong love of herps with her professional training as a board-certified diplomate in the American College of Veterinary Nutrition. She has written more than 50 publications in peer-reviewed scientific journals and more than 100 chapters and articles on nutrition and health. She has served as editor for several publications and as president of the American Academy of Veterinary Nutrition. She owns Nutrition Support Services, Inc., designs and markets the Walkabout Farm line of dietary products for herps, and is an avid breeder of bearded dragons.

Roger Klingenberg, DVM, has had a lifelong passion for reptiles, which inspired his pursuit of a veterinary degree from Colorado State University. His combined skills of veterinary specialization in treating reptiles, along with more than 30 years of experience in keeping and breeding a variety of lizards, snakes, and turtles, have helped bring him to the forefront of reptile veterinary medicine and surgery. He has shared his extensive knowledge and experience through lectures, magazine articles, textbook chapters, and scientific papers. He is the author of *Understanding Reptile Parasites* and coauthor of several best-selling books on reptile care, including *The Box Turtle Manual*, *The Ball Python Manual*, and *The Boa Constrictor Manual*.

Jerry Cole is an experienced herpetoculturist who has kept and bred reptiles since the early 1980s. In 1984, he and his wife, Belinda, formed B.J. Herp Supplies. Over the years, they developed many new reptile-oriented products, the best known probably being Nature's Image T-shirts. They run their business from purpose-built facilities on their farm in South West England and supply captive-bred livestock, equipment, and literature to pet stores and hobbyists throughout Europe.

Susan M. Ewing (technical editor, 3rd edition) is an award-winning author of numerous animal books and magazine articles as well as a weekly newspaper column about pets that ran for twenty years. She is a member of several professional associations for pet writers and was inducted into the Dog Writers' Hall of Fame in 2021. She lives in Jamestown, New York, with her husband, Jim, and two Corgis, Gael and Tegan.

Terri M. Sommella (technical editor, 2nd edition) is a life-long herpetoculturist and the owner of Fire and Ice Dragons, formed in 1998. She was the first to promote reptile pedigrees, drawing attention to the importance of record-keeping. Her articles on bearded dragons have appeared in such publications as *Reptiles Magazine* and *Practical Reptile Keeping*. Fire and Ice's beautiful Super Citrus color morph was voted Best of the Best Reptile over fifteen years. She continues to emphasize not only gorgeous colors in her lines but also the importance of breeding for vigor and true size.